PINS ON A MAP

PINS ON A MAP

A Family's Yearlong Journey Around the World

BY DAVID BOESCH

REEDY PRESS
St. Louis, Missouri

For my family. You mean the world to me.

Reedy Press
PO Box 5131
St. Louis, MO 63139, USA

Library of Congress Control Number: 2010931678

ISBN: 978-1-933370-68-2

Please visit our website at www.reedypress.com.

Design by Jill Halpin

Printed in the United States of America
10 11 12 13 14   5 4 3 2 1

CONTENTS

1. PLACING PINS: Why Travel Matters   1

2. PREPARATIONS: Remember to Pack Pencils   7

3. NORTH AMERICA: Pulling Your Weight   14

4. PIZZA: Finding Old-World Culture Close to Home   27

5. AFRICA: Balance in the Serengeti   33

6. EUROPE: Behind the Wheel   49

7. TURKEY: Hitting Our Stride among Friends   59

8. INDIA: A Bout of Culture Shock   91

9. THAILAND: A Family Lost, a Family Found   106

10. JAPAN: Cami's Broken Leg   116

11. AUSTRALIA: Sex Education in an RV   126

12. NEW ZEALAND: "Doon't Look Doon" and Other Extreme Sports   136

13. ARGENTINA: Food Good; Salsa Man Bad   142

14. CHILE: A Simple Day Hike   150

15. HOME AT LAST: Untold Tales, Lessons Learned, Lives Changed   159

Acknowledgments   169

Bibliography   171

Pizza Results   173

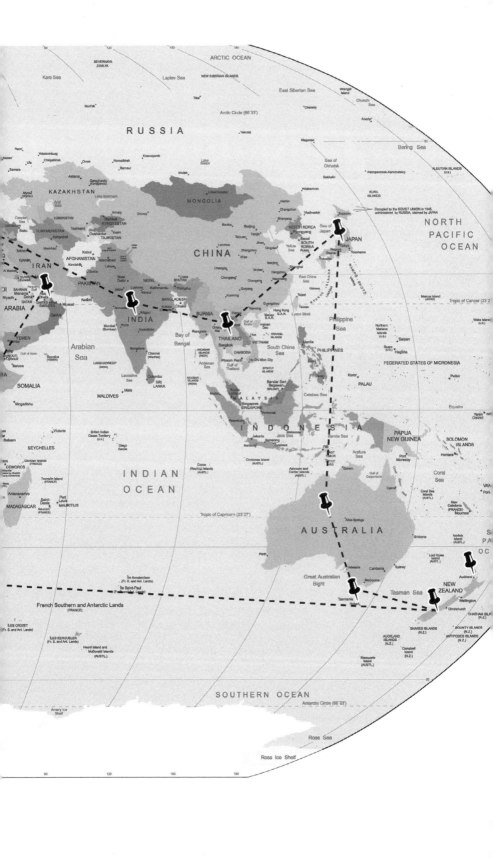

CHAPTER 1

PLACING PINS

Why Travel Matters |

*S*n 1993 my bride, Jill, and I took a trip to Nepal for a month of hiking in the Himalayas. We didn't climb Mount Everest, but we did scale some big peaks, including the 18,200-foot-high Kala Pattar.

We both got sick in Nepal. I came down with an intestinal parasite, and Jill developed a serious condition called high altitude cerebral edema. Her brain was swollen, which caused headaches, an inability to walk, and confusion. From a medical standpoint, we recovered, but we were never the same after that trip.

Our experience in Nepal changed us. It was an adventure, not a vacation, and despite the hardships—or perhaps because of them—we found ourselves talking about taking an even bigger trip, a trip around the world, a dream that soon became known simply as "the trip." We talked about these things as we lay awake every night until 3 a.m., trying to overcome our jet lag.

Ten months later, we had our first child, a boy. "*Ringpoche*," a very popular Tibetan Buddhist name, was my choice, but Jill won out and we called our son Joseph. In 1998, we had our second child, Thomas, and shortly thereafter we had a daughter, Camilla. For obvious reasons, we didn't talk much about the trip anymore. We both assumed that we would get back to that dream after we had retired and life had slowed down.

We spent summers in a little cabin in Ketchikan, Alaska, and the rest of the year we lived in Mesa, Arizona. From time to time, we traveled with the kids. We had reached the point in life where we marked the passage of time by the ages of our children. Each December, Jill and I looked back at the previous year, and each December we found ourselves saying the same thing: "The time flew by so fast. Where did that year go?" Even with the aid of notes on the calendar, most of the events and occasions of the year just past were impossible to recollect.

Yet some events and occasions we remembered vividly—times of such clarity that our minds seemed to be recording in high definition. Most of these times, we realized, occurred while we were on the road. Long weekends in Flagstaff or Tucson created memories just as rich as bigger trips to Montana. What mattered was that we were together as a family, exploring a new place. Travel for us was life lived under the microscope, with bigger joys and bigger disappointments than we experienced in everyday life. Passion springs from newness, and the shifting landscape of travel made us more alive, more aware.

In December 2003, Jill looked at me and said, "I think we should take the trip with the kids. It would be a tremendous education for them, and it would transform the trip from a selfish endeavor to an unselfish one."

I loved the idea. A trip of this nature would be all too easy to keep putting off "until we don't have quite as much going on." And quite likely each year would bring a new reason for further procrastination. Deciding to bring the kids also gave us the very special gift of a deadline. We now had to travel at the best time based on the ages of our children. If we made the trip too early, they might not remember it. Too late, and they might be in the petulant teen stage where they would be more interested in texting their BFFs than in touring the Louvre. After much discussion, we decided the ideal time to leave would be May 2007. Cami would be seven, Tommy ten, and Joey thirteen.

I planned a special occasion to tell the boys, who were then six and ten. On a backpacking trip to Horton Springs, over a campfire I explained that we would take off for a year and go around the world. I said we could visit any country we were interested in. I asked Joe where he would like to go. "Paris and Mongolia," he said. "I really like Genghis Khan, and I want to see where he is from."

Tommy said he wanted to visit Texas. I asked him why. He had a ready answer: "That's where Sandy from Sponge Bob is from! Don't you know anything?"

People have traveled around the world since 1520. Portuguese Captain Ferdinand Magellan got credit for being the first, though he was not. Sailing under the Spanish flag, he began the voyage in 1519, with four ships and 250 men. After discovering the straits that now bear his name and sailing across a huge swath of the Pacific, Magellan arrived in the Philippines.

All that was left to do was sail home to Spain—an easy trip. Then, in a remarkable act that combined religious grandiosity with colonial hubris, Magellan decided to attack a primitive tribe that refused to convert to Catholicism. While wading ashore in waist-deep water, Magellan was stoned and stabbed to death by the Philippine Chief Lapu Lapu. The chief's victory is celebrated each year on National Heroes Day in the Philippines.

Juan Sebastian Del Cano, a Basque sailor on the journey with Magellan, returned to Spain with one ship and seventeen surviving crew members.

So yes, people have traveled around the world before—but could we? Jill and I wrestled with three key questions:

1. Could we plan and execute the travel? Even though neither Jill nor I had been out of the country in fourteen years, we felt good about our chances here.

2. Could we afford it? If we cashed in everything except our house and took out a home equity loan, we would have $140,000 for a year, or $400 a day. That seemed like enough. We would minimize expensive destinations like Europe and maximize cheaper ones such as Asia and South America.

3. Could the five of us get along sharing close quarters for a year? That question troubled us the most.

The kids were far apart in age and had widely varied interests. Cami loves animals. Tommy plays the guitar and has a circle of close friends. Joe enjoys computers and history. Many of the activities we hoped to do might interest one, but not all three. At home they could each go their separate ways, but on the road a lot of compromise would be required.

We get along pretty well as a family, but we are not without our differences. We worried that travel would magnify these differences. We wondered if our family dynamic would disintegrate over time.

One week after the backpacking trip with the boys, we took the St. Louis Cardinals pennant off our office wall (I love the Redbirds, so this was a big deal) and put in its place the biggest laminated map of the world we could find—a map that measured seventy-two by forty-seven inches. We stuck thumbtacks in places we wanted to go. Italy got my first thumbtack, Jill stuck hers on Nepal.

A few days later, Jill bought pins in different colors that worked better than thumbtacks. We began sticking the pins in the map. We put orange pins where we knew people or knew people who knew people. We stuck red pins in places we definitely wanted to go. White pins were used for possible destinations.

The kids would come home from school and stare at the map. Joey put pins in Mongolia and Paris. Tommy was learning about South America in school, so he stuck pins in Ecuador and Argentina. Cami, just four, could barely reach the bottom of the map. She didn't really understand what the boys were doing, but she didn't want to be left out, so Cami put pins in Antarctica and the Southern Ocean.

Jill and I stopped saving for college and began saving for the trip, investing heavily in the stock market. I had this fantasy that we wouldn't tell anybody about our travels until the week before we departed. Then, when the bell rang at the end of the last day of the school year, we would pick up the kids and drive away. I imagined our friends lining the roads like on Palm Sunday in Jerusalem, waving and throwing roses—only instead of a donkey, we would be riding a minivan. When people would ask, "How long will you be gone," we would yell, "We'll be home when we get back."

The reality was that we had to tell some people. We told our families. My mom died in 1993, and I am an only child. My father, Edward Boesch, spends winters in Arizona and the rest of the year in St. Louis, his lifelong home. Even as an adult, I sought his approval. When I told him of our plans he looked at me in silence. After a long pause, he said, "If you really want to do something like that, David, Disney has Epcot Center. We took you there when you were twelve."

In fact, most of my boyhood vacations were to Florida, usually during the summer. My dad continued, "They have pavilions on lots of countries so you can go around the world without having to leave America. It would be safer too, and a hell of a lot cheaper."

In June 2004, I approached my boss, who also is a good friend. "Jill and I are going to take the kids around the world in 2007," I said. "I wanted to give you fair notice so that you can hire someone to take my place." Our contract requires six months' notice, but I figured three years was better.

Chris knew me well enough to know that I wasn't joking, but I don't think he believed we would actually do it. He said, "I can't promise anything, but I am hopeful we will have a place for you when you return." Then he gave me a one hundred dollar bill to put in my wallet in case of an emergency.

After speaking to our parents and to Chris, we decided to keep our plans to ourselves. We had contingency plans in case someone in the family got sick or something else went wrong, and we didn't want to be thought of as people who talked big about what they were going to do but lacked the perseverance to see it through. Every person we informed would mean a further degree of com- mitment, as well as another person to explain ourselves to if we decided to stay home.

Our next decision pertained to our house. I wanted to sell it. The romance of cashing in all our chips and heading off into the sunset appealed to me. I also thought that selling the house would teach the kids about the unimportance of material things and the illusion of stability in our lives.

Jill felt that the kids needed a home to return to. By "home" she did not simply mean bricks and mortar (in Arizona, our home was built of stucco) but a place of comfort and routine that the kids could dream about when times got tough. Tommy and Cami insisted that we not sell the house. They liked their school and their routines. Joe didn't care.

We decided not to sell, but we couldn't afford to let our house sit empty. We needed the rental income and someone to pay the utilities. We also needed someone in the house to care for our two dogs, Slinky and Cookie. As luck would have it, a relative and her family were looking to move to Arizona, and they liked dogs. They agreed to watch our dogs, and in exchange, we rented our home to them below market value.

Next, we learned that if you lease a car, it is possible to hand it in anywhere in the United States, so we leased a minivan with a special tow package so that the lease would expire when we were ready to leave the country.

So far, so good.

On September 15, 2004, I was at work in the Emergency Department when one of our secretaries paged me over the loudspeaker about a call. Nothing unusual about that—it happens all the time. The call was from a neurosurgeon who told me that my father had been in an accident.

Apparently, my dad had driven to the hardware store. When he changed lanes, he ran into the back of a Dr. Pepper truck. His car didn't have much damage, but he immediately became a quadriplegic. He underwent surgery and had six months of physical therapy, but unfortunately he made no improvement.

I told my dad we would move our family back to St. Louis to be with him (Jill was in favor of this as well), but he decided to come to Arizona. We planned on using money we had saved for the trip to build an accessible addition to our home. When the kids asked if the trip was off, we said that it was. To our surprise, they seemed to understand. We stopped sticking pins in the map.

Because my father had medical needs that Jill and I couldn't take care of until the addition was completed, we found a private home for him. By January 2005, when my father realized he would never walk again, he lost both his appetite and his will to live. Shortly after 10 p.m. on February 19, the phone rang. The owner of the group home called to say that my dad had taken a sudden turn for the worse.

I jumped in the car and sped through the pouring rain. When I arrived, he was unconscious and breathing irregularly. I held his hand and prayed silently. In seventeen years as a doctor, I had seen this many times, and I knew he would soon be dead. At least he wouldn't be alone.

Suddenly, I felt my dad's right thumb—the only thing he could move with much strength—squeeze my hand.

"Hi Dave," he said.

"Hi Dad," I replied, shocked that he had woken up. "Dad, it's time."

"I know."

"Do you want to go to the hospital?"

"No."

"Do you want some water?"

"No thanks."

" I love you, Dad. I appreciate all the sacrifices you made for me."

"Good. I love you too."

"Do you want to say some prayers?"

"Yeah."

We made it through an Our Father and a Hail Mary. Then he breathed his last.

I would love to say that we made our trip in honor of my father, that it was always his dream to go around the world and that we lived it for him. That would be untrue. My father was a good man: unselfish, honest, faithful, and practical. His idea of a good time was a round of golf with his friends. A trip around the world is something he never would have considered.

CHAPTER 2

PREPARATIONS

Remember to Pack Pencils |

*P*ins slowly began making their way back into the map.

Safety was our first concern as we winnowed down our list of destinations. Almost everyone knows someone who knows someone else who was robbed in Buenos Aires or mugged in Istanbul. The conclusion deduced from this kind of anecdotal evidence is that those places must be dangerous, that you should never go there—especially with kids.

Assumptions such as this are not peculiar to foreign travel. A few years ago a friend and his family were coming to visit us in Alaska during the summer. He asked, "Should I bring my biggest gun in case we run into a bear?"

The better question would be: "What do people die from in the Alaska wilderness?" Data reveal that from 2000 to 2005 there were 182 deaths in the Alaska wilderness. Eighty were due to drowning and three were due to bear mauling. Those three deaths, of course, were page-one national news stories. Death due to bear mauling is truly awful, widely reported, and incredibly rare. Drowning was twenty-five times more common but reported only locally. In other words, if you want to survive in the Alaska wilderness bring a life preserver, not your biggest gun.

How rational were our fears regarding international travel? Were we worried about "bears" when we should have been worried about "drowning"? This is an emotional topic, but we wanted to approach it in an analytical way. We asked ourselves these questions:

"What bad things are so awful that we would never forgive ourselves if they occurred?"

"What bad things are likely to happen?"

"What bad things, in either category, can we prevent?"

The truly awful things we came up with were airplane crash, murder, and kidnapping. We began to look for data. We learned that the odds of being killed while on an airplane flight are 1 in 10.46 million if you are traveling on one of the world's 25 safest airlines. (We had heard of nearly all of these airlines.) The odds increase by more than a hundredfold (to 1 in 723,819) if you are on one of the world's 25 least safe airlines. (We had heard of none of these airlines.) So we resolved that if we had not heard of an airline, we would not fly on it.

The World Health Organization publishes data on murder per capita as expressed in murders per 100,000 citizens per year: Japan is 0.4; the U.S. rate is 4; South Africa is 39. We removed the pin from South Africa.

We were unable to find reliable data regarding child abduction, but we taught our kids to yell, "These are not my parents," if they were grabbed, and to do all they could to stay put and make their stand in a public place.

As a family, we planned to take self-defense classes. I harbored an illusion that we could become a family of ninjas, ready to take on anyone who messed with us. We would learn to fight together as a team, and we would each have our own signature move and special fighting skill, like in the movie *The Incredibles*.

Jill was the only one who followed through. She took an intensive three-day self-defense class. On the third day she came home, looked me in the eyes, and said, "Grab me from behind." In fifteen years of marriage she never had to say that twice. The next thing I knew I was lying flat on my back in front of the TV (*SportsCenter* was on), and Jill had the heel of her pointy boot pressed tight over my throat.

I smiled up at her. "That was such a turn-on. Can you do it again?"

The more research we did, the clearer it became that the bad things likely to happen to us were sickness, car crashes, and theft—all things that we could influence through preparation, medication, or alteration of our behavior.

We visited a travel medicine specialist to get vaccines and anti-malaria tablets. We purchased a water purifier. I assembled a first-aid kit and portable pharmacy that would treat common conditions such as lacerations, jet lag, and strep throat. We bought the best travel health insurance we could find. The policy included a flight home for advanced medical care if we needed it, and it even paid for "return of remains" in case the very worst happened.

Data on vehicle fatalities and serious crashes per mile are available. There are places where driving is incredibly dangerous. Egypt is one of them, and so that pin came out of the map. We vowed that we would only travel in cars with seat belts and always travel together in the same vehicle.

Because street crime is so common in so many places, we simply assumed that sometime during the year ahead, we would be robbed. This didn't bother us. Part of the lesson we wanted to teach our kids is that not everyone in the world is nice. A minor theft (a suitcase, an iPod) would teach that lesson. Our passports were the only thing we were not prepared to have stolen, so we planned to keep them either in the hotel safe or in a zippered and buttoned pocket on the front of my shirt.

Once countries had passed our "safety test," we made choices based on culture, cost, and climate. We subscribed to travel magazines that had many articles on "luxury cruises" and "five star resorts" but few on "budget family travel." We read these magazines, but we didn't trust them. The magazines seem to exist to drum up business for their advertisers.

We watched travel DVDs. Jill and the kids were particularly interested in places that were beautiful or interesting. I was interested in places that were cheap. When a narrator on a DVD would say ". . . and hotels only cost ten dollars," I would quickly run to the map and stick in a new pin.

By September 2006, we had about forty pins in the map. We ordered travel books for many of these destinations. These books were meant to promote travel, but they often had the opposite effect and convinced us not to visit. Some of the best money we spent was in buying travel books for places we did not go. Greenland was too expensive. Mongolia was too hard to get to. (Joe took the news in stride.)

We wanted to avoid extremes of hot and cold and aim for "sweater weather"—between 50 and 70 degrees—in every country. Even families that get along well tend to get short-tempered in hot, muggy weather. We studied *Times Books: The World Weather Guide,* by E. A. Pearce, a great resource that details monthly temperature and rainfall for every country in the world. We tore out sections from the countries we were considering and listed what months would have ideal weather. Then we tried to put the countries in order. This required sacrificing more coveted destinations: Nepal (too cold), Russia (too cold), and New Guinea (too hot).

The Practical Nomad: How to Travel Around the World, by Edward Hasbrouck, was a big help when it came to arranging finances, planning a budget, and taking care of financial matters at home. The book also helped us decide how to arrange our international airline reservations: There are many options. The least expensive and least flexible involved purchasing tickets from a ticket consolidator. These "bucket shops" buy unused international tickets in bulk and sell them at a discount. After we decided to buy tickets from a consolidator, we had to put our destinations in order. We could only buy tickets up to six months ahead of our departure date, so we only had to organize the first ten or so countries. This sounds easy, but it proved to be like putting together the pieces of a puzzle that never quite fit.

Africa was our first stumbling block. If you fly from the United States to Europe to Asia to Australia/New Zealand to South America and back to the United States, you've flown almost in a straight line (check it out on a globe). No matter how you draw the line, Africa is out of the way, and getting there is expensive. I pleaded with Jill to drop Africa as a destination, but she wouldn't budge.

We needed to be in Africa in the dry season, when animals gather around watering holes and are easier to spot. Once the rainy season comes, the animals disperse, the roads wash out, and the risk of malaria increases. We could have gone straight from New York to Africa, which would have put us there in September (dry season), but we didn't want to make Africa our first international stop. Jet lag is more difficult on children than on adults, and we didn't want tired kids riding around in the safari vehicles during the day and staying awake in the tent all night. A stop in England was the means to our end. We were scheduled to change planes en route to Tanzania anyway, and England was in the same time zone, which would solve our jet lag concern.

Many other decisions were just as difficult. None were perfect—nearly all required compromise. Our route north from Tanzania took us through Dubai. A flight from Dubai to Delhi was easy and cheap, but that would have meant skipping continental Europe. The other more expensive option was to fly from Dubai to France and then work our way East. (This is what we eventually decided to do.) We agonized over these decisions. In addition to choosing and ordering our destinations, we also had to decide how much time we were going to spend in each place. This was pure guesswork.

The kids were excited when we talked about travel, but they were more excited by the mistaken assumption that they would be skipping a year of school. Jill and I wanted the kids to receive school credit for the year we spent on the road, and that meant that we would need to teach them.

To help ourselves become better educators, we took substitute teacher training. My first substitute gig was kindergarten music. It was fun. We sang a song about turtles. My next assignment was Joe's sixth-grade classroom. I had ample notice that I would be substituting, and so I had time to formulate a lesson plan.

"Watch out for Nathan," was all Joe said as he mounted his bike and prepared to leave for school.

"How are you going to introduce yourself to the class?" Jill asked as I was on my way out the door.

"Mr. Boesch," I replied.

"Not Dr. Boesch?" she asked.

"I don't need to hide behind that title."

"These are sixth graders," she said. "They won't respect you just because."

"Oh, yes they will," I replied, "or there will be hell to pay."

Joe's classroom adjoined another. The teacher in the adjoining room offered to help me if I had any problems. Things got off to a good start. The first subject was science. After an hour, kids started leaving to go to the bathroom at an alarming rate. It was either a cholera outbreak or they were messing with me.

"What does your teacher usually do when you need to use the restroom?" I asked the class.

"She lets us go whenever we want," replied a short kid with a thin nose and spiky black hair. This was Nathan.

I looked over at Joe. His head was down, and he refused to make eye contact. I understood. He didn't want to be seen as a snitch so he wasn't going to let on as to what his regular teacher would have done. I decided to nip Nathan's behavior in the bud. "Well, I say no one else can go to the bathroom for another half hour."

"But I really have to go. Poop, if you need to know," Nathan said while standing up from his chair and pretending to squirm. The class burst out laughing.

"I don't need to know, and you can sit down," I replied.

He sat down and put his hood over his head, Eminem style.

"Take your hood off," I ordered.

He said, "I'm only wearing it because I really have to go to the bathroom."

I wondered whether he tormented substitutes like this before. He was pretty good at it. "Outside," I bellowed, pointing to the door.

Once outside the classroom I let Nathan know that I would not tolerate his insolence. I was businesslike, but inside I was furious at the surprising realization that here stood a student not the least bit interested in learning. I did not threaten to send him to the principal's office or call his parents, thinking that those tactics were reserved for teachers who did not command respect.

My talk with Nathan worked—for all of fifteen minutes, after which time our verbal jousting resumed. He put his hand up. I refused to call on him. He scooted his desk back and forth. I made him turn around and face away from the class. He began making fart noises.

The teacher from the adjoining classroom must have heard the commotion, because he motioned for me to come over to the door. "He's not a bad kid. He just knows that there is no consequence in misbehaving for a teacher that won't be here tomorrow. Why don't I just take him in my class for the rest of the day?"

"That is probably for the best," I replied, all the while wishing I was singing about turtles with the kindergarteners. Thus ended my brief career as a substitute teacher.

That night at dinner, accompanied by a stiff vodka and tonic, I lamented that a sixth grader got the better of me. In an attempt to cheer me up, Joe said, "Don't be so hard on yourself, Dad. You did way better than the last three subs."

This was Joe's final year of grade school. Upon returning from our year of travel, he would be transferring to a new charter school. At the school orientation, we introduced ourselves to the headmaster and explained our plan to travel around the world. We said we hoped that Joe would be accepted as an eighth grader when we returned from the trip. The headmaster quickly recognized the educational value of our adventure and said it would be his pleasure to give Joe credit for our year of travel, and to welcome him back as an eighth grader.

Joe would be expected to make academic progress while we were on the road, and he would be tested in math and Latin when we returned. If he came up short in either, he would need to attend summer school. I was excited to teach math, but I didn't know a thing about Latin except that the textbooks were quite heavy and took up a lot of room in the luggage.

The principal at Cami and Tommy's school—she was in second grade and he was in fourth—advised us to call the school district home-school adviser and notify him of our travel plans. When we spoke with the home-school adviser, he said that upon our return the kids would be placed in the appropriate grade, as though they hadn't missed any school at all. There was no need for testing. By being a year older, they would get credit for being a year smarter! If problems arose when they re-enrolled we would deal with them at that time.

This same man said, "The most I would bring along from an educational point of view is a math book and a pencil. Math is the one subject that builds upon itself. Travel will take care of the rest." I rejoiced. "A math book and a pencil"—this was Zen-like simplicity. I loved the wise man from the school district, but Jill thought his advice made things seem too easy. She could not bring herself to overlook penmanship and grammar. Jill talked with experienced home-school parents. She sent away for home-school books. She investigated computer-based curricula. I argued that information technology went hand-in-hand with unreliability.

Pencils, on the other hand, represent reliable technology. They are elegantly designed to be held in your hand and then lay down a thin layer of graphite whenever they are applied to paper. They may break on occasion, but (and this is the key) that break is easily fixable by someone without expert knowledge regarding their design and manufacture. I trust pencils completely.

We did not completely ignore technology. Jill decided that a website would be a good idea. By December 2006, www.boeschfamilytravels.com was up and running. Our Christmas cards that year notified our friends and family about our website and served as our formal announcement regarding our upcoming journey. The response to our Christmas cards was unpredictable and, I believe, represents the wide variation of feelings people have when it comes to travel. Some of our closest friends were silent while some distant acquaintances became enamored with the trip and were frequently in touch. A few expressed concerns that we would do something fraught with danger, "especially with the kids."

After setting up the website, we asked Joe, Tommy, and Cami to begin keeping journals to document their emotions regarding the trip. They didn't. We soon realized that broad-based writing assignments are often more difficult than specific ones. We learned to say, "For the next half hour, write about the place you are most afraid of," as opposed to "Write about your feelings regarding the trip."

By January 2007, plans were in high gear. It was still possible to cancel—but barring some major emergency, we were going. Packing was a cinch. The trick was to not care about your personal appearance. This was never a problem for me.

The week before departure was frenetic. Sometimes Jill and I would be working together, but a lot of times we were working separately. Our styles of getting things done differ. Hers involves a lot of time on the phone; mine takes a lot of time on the computer. We both knew that each of us were doing the best we could in our own way. We made it through the final week of preparation without a single fight.

On May 31, 2007, we were up at 5 a.m. Leaving for the trip and renting our house had forced us to go through all of our stuff and to get rid of what we didn't need. What we kept, we moved into Tommy's old room, which was now functioning as our storage room. I borrowed a trailer and dropped a huge load at the dump. A phalanx of maids arrived to clean the house, and only Jill was allowed back in. The kids and I finished loading the camper. Then we sat in the hot garage, waiting for Jill, waiting to begin our trip around the world.

CHAPTER 3

NORTH AMERIC.

Pulling Your Weight | *May 31–September 12, 2007*

or five years, we had been dreaming of this day. We spent the morning of May 31, 2007, packing up the house and saying farewell to friends. We had a farewell toast of sparkling cider in our driveway. Cami explained our trip to the dogs, telling them every country we were going to visit and also when we would be back. We then waved goodbye to our neighbors and set off to see the world.

From Joey's journal:

The big day is finally here. I guess it sort of came up pretty quick. In the last few months the trip has seemed like it would never come, and today we still have a lot to do.

Driving north past Saguaro Lake, we were treated to a gorgeous sunset as Willie Nelson sang on the car CD player. I always imagined it just like this; the five of us with teary eyes, sad to be leaving home yet filled with awe about the magnitude of our adventure. It was one of those rare moments that should have been full of grandeur. But there was no awe, no feeling that we were embarking on some grand quest. All we felt was relief and irritation. Relief that we were finally on the road and irritation that the kids were already bickering over what DVD they were going to watch. We were tired, too. Fortunately, our first stop on our trip around the world was a mere one hundred miles away at Woods Canyon Lake, Arizona.

We have done a lot of backpacking, but this was our family's first camper experience. Our "rig" was a 19-foot, 3,400-pound, hard-sided travel trailer with queen fold-out beds at the front and back. It had a refrigerator, stove, heater, and microwave. We pulled this with our 2005 Toyota Sienna van, which has a V-6 motor, a towing capacity of 3,500 pounds, and a special strap-on mirror so we could see around the trailer. Keeping the trip in mind, we had carefully nursed the van during the previous three years so that it only had 25,500 miles on a lease that was good for 36,000—hopefully enough to get us across the country.

The van was equipped with a sensor that tells you in real time what mileage your vehicle is getting. Without the trailer, the read-out typically was between 20 and 26 miles per gallon, but pulling the trailer up our first big hill, it read "2." Gas cost $3 per gallon, and it dawned on me that the eight-mile hill we had just ascended cost us $12.

We pulled into Woods Canyon Lake after dark and found a campsite. I tried to back up the trailer, but it kept jackknifing. Jill was patiently coaching me, but I finally gave up. She hopped in and backed it right down the center of the campsite on her first try.

After two days of catching crawdads and drinking beer, we drove away from the campground and headed for the cool climate of Colorado. We were traveling west near Grand Junction when a tire blew on the trailer. It fishtailed off to the left a bit, but we managed to pull over and no one was hurt. I went to get the spare off the back side of the trailer. It was a hot day and the kids were still in the air-conditioned car. I expect most wives would have been right there with them, but not Jill. By the time I returned with the spare, she had loosened the lug nuts and was commencing to crank up the jack. In Durango, we learned that it was a bad idea to take the camper through the drive-through at Wendy's, even though the overhead clearance was ten feet and our trailer was only eight feet. The corners were too tight and the wheels got stuck.

I got out of the van and tried to explain to the drivers who were seven deep in line behind us that they would need to move so Jill could back us up. Those drivers were not understanding and not the least bit interested that I was a rookie vis-à-vis recreational vehicles. They wanted crispy chicken sandwiches, and we were in the way. One went so far as to roll up his window while I was in mid-sentence.

On a two-lane road near the Bonneville Salt Flats in Utah, I noticed an old wooden sign bearing the words "Fossils, you dig" with an arrow underneath pointing down a dirt road. I hit the brakes. Long road trips tend to hypnotize Jill, and in a sleepy voice she asked, "Why are you stopping?"

I replied, "I wonder if that sign should have a question mark."

She slowly read the sign and shook her head. "Just get going."

"Let's check this out," I said. "It could be fun." We turned onto the narrow dirt road and began to drive. Pulling the trailer, it was hard to go more than twenty miles per hour. The next sign read, "Fossils 12 miles." It became clear that at this rate digging for fossils was going to be a three-hour endeavor. The road was also getting worse, but I found a wide spot and pulled the van over again.

"Just turn around and go back," Jill said.

"What's going on?" Tommy asked.

"Your dad, the rock hound, wants to drive two hours up this road to look for fossils."

It's true. I am a rock hound. I used to collect rocks with my dad when I was a kid and I remember how much fun we had looking for geodes. I thought the kids would enjoy it too, so I made them turn off the overhead DVD player while I pled my case about why it would be fun to dig for fossils. We then made a democratic family decision. The vote was 4–1.

"Sorry, rock hound," Jill said with a laugh. "Maybe next time."

Driving across the deserted roads of Utah and then Nevada, I wondered for hours about what we may have missed. The decision not to look for fossils was more nuanced than it seemed. On the one hand, we were hours from nowhere and a flat tire on the dirt road would have been a disaster. It was also getting late in the day and a three-hour sojourn would mean "dry camping" with no water or bathroom. Last but not least, it was Sunday in Utah, which meant that the purveyors of "Fossils, you dig" were probably in church all day if they were like most of the Mormons we know. The place could have been closed when we finally arrived.

On the other hand, we could have learned about geology and found some awesome fossils—our geologic link with earth's earlier life forms. So it was adventure versus the practical. In this case, practical won out, for good reason. We make decisions like this every day, of course, but on the road they seem bigger—life under a microscope. I wondered how many similar decisions we would be faced with over the next year.

From Utah we made our way to Yosemite National Park, where the boys and I went on a backpacking trip. The mosquitoes in Yosemite were horrible, and even though we were well prepared, it made for some real misery. Tommy wished death to all mosquitoes on earth. I told him the insects are an important part of the food chain, and that before he made such a wish, he should learn more about them. That led to the first school assignment of the trip: Tommy's Mosquito Report. Here is an excerpt:

Many animals eat mosquitoes. Frogs and some birds eat mosquitoes, so do bats. Dragonflies are great mosquito eaters. If you look into a dragonfly's mouth you can see up to 100 mosquitoes.

All mosquitoes eat flower pollen. Female mosquitoes drink animal's blood for the protein they need to make eggs. This is how they spread disease. Mosquitoes spread malaria, yellow fever and west Nile virus. These diseases spread by mosquitoes kill millions of people each year many of whom are children under the age of five.

In conclusion I still wish all mosquitoes were dead.

We were off to the Pacific Northwest. Whenever we pulled into a trailer park, the boys helped me unhook the trailer from the hitch, plug it in, and attach the water hose. When we first started, the whole process took fifteen minutes, but after a few weeks we were down to five minutes, even in the dark. It would have been faster but a wire near the hitch kept getting in the way. I told Joe to pull out the wire and throw it away. The following day we slept late. When we awoke, we were in an empty campground. We hooked the camper up, but its tires wouldn't roll. They were locked in place and skidded along as though the brake was still on.

I checked it out and everything looked fine. Perhaps I needed to pull harder to get the tires unstuck. I put the van in first gear and dragged the camper about ten feet through the grass. The transmission on the van didn't like that and started to slip. I briefly thought about trying to pull the camper to Vermont in that condition but realized it would be impossible. I went to the campground office to find the phone number of a mechanic.

Just as I returned, a family pulled into the spot next to us. Jill spoke with the driver and explained our problem. Yes, he knew a lot about trailers. He had pulled them thirty years. Sure, he would be happy to have a look at ours.

"Where's your emergency brake cable?" he asked.

"What's that?" I said.

"It's the cable that causes your brakes to lock when it is pulled out. That way if your trailer becomes unhooked from the car, it automatically stops instead of careening out of control." He showed me the emergency brake cable on his rig. It looked exactly like the wire I had told Joey to throw away.

I thanked the guy and whispered to Joe to dive in the dumpster and pull it out. Joe gave me a dirty look, but he went. While he was dumpster diving, Jill found the wire in our trash can.

Even with the high price of fuel, the camper still saved a lot of money. The cost of an RV park is a fraction of a hotel room, and many campgrounds are exempt from occupancy taxes that municipalities tack onto your hotel bill. Having a camper also saved money on food. For years, Jill and I have said, "Instead of eating out, we'll buy a cooler and go shopping—then we'll eat in the hotel room." We never did. With a camper, we always had easy access to a refrigerator full of food and drinks—not to mention a bathroom.

The camper came equipped with a smoke detector that seemed to go off every time Jill cooked dinner. It also came equipped with a carbon monoxide detector that emitted a high-pitched screech whenever it detected CO. The detector was quiet at first, but after a couple of weeks it began sounding the alarm in the middle of the night, waking up all of us.

The kids insisted that the alarm was actually a "fart detector," and they blamed me for setting it off. I could not deny my flatulence, but I did try to argue that fart gas does not contain CO in any appreciable concentration. They remained unconvinced. On top of the CO detector was a sticker that read, "Do not disable," but we were tired of being awakened every night. The sticker itself took a while to remove. Getting the detector open was much easier. Inside were a red wire and a white wire, both leading to the alarm. Which wire should we cut? We couldn't decide, so we cut both, and never heard from the CO detector again.

The rest of the family slept quietly as I drove north along the Pacific Coast. I saw a sign with a left arrow that read "blueberries for sale." I love blueberries. We were going pretty fast, so I slammed on the brakes and pulled the trailer into a little driveway lined with trees and bushes. The quick turn didn't wake anyone, but the tree branches smacking the side of the camper did. The blueberry sellers must have heard us too, because they ran out to us with blueberries. After selling us six boxes, they encouraged me to not bring the RV farther into their driveway. I tried backing out, but once again the trailer kept jackknifing. Jill took over the driver's seat.

Farther north, we visited a replica of Fort Clatsop, where Lewis and Clark spent the winter before returning East. This was our first museum stop of the trip, and it was a rainy day. Nearby was a monument marking where a Japanese artillery shell hit the Washington State Beach during World War II. Heading there, we turned down a dirt road that became more and more narrow and then turned to sand—very wet sand. The trailer began to slide, and it was clear we were going to get stuck. There were no other cars around.

As with the fossils, the vote was 4–1 against taking this trip, but this time we went anyway. When we came to a wide spot in the road, I stopped the van. I told Jill I was going to look for a better place to turn around, but I was secretly planning to run up and look at the monument. In the pouring rain, I arrived at the beach to find two big poles topped with orange flags marking the spot where the shell had hit—not much of a monument.

I ran back to the car. I told Jill that the wide spot in the road in front of us was as good as we were going to get. While I had been at the beach, she had come up with a plan. She thought we could make it if I put the van in first gear, floored it, and turned quickly around. We hoped that the trailer would fishtail as the van turned hard left. "Whatever you do, David, don't stop, because if you do we will be stuck for sure," cautioned Jill. I tried talking her into driving, but she refused. "No way. You are the only one in this family nerdy enough to want to come here, you get us out."

I put the van in first gear and tried peeling out, but the wheels dug deeper into the sand. I tried going slower. As the van slowly moved forward, I shifted to second and picked up speed, keeping it in second. I turned the van hard to the left and knocked off the strap on the mirror on the passenger side. I felt the trailer slide behind us and pull hard to starboard. It worked—we were now moving back in the right direction.

In Seattle, we decided to take a break from camper life and enjoy the city. We called a downtown hotel and got permission to back the trailer into their parking garage where maintenance vehicles and delivery trucks parked. The man at the hotel neglected to mention the low clearance, and our antenna scraped noisily against the ceiling, but Jill backed the trailer into the basement of our hotel without a problem.

Three days later, we tried to pull it up the ramp. Halfway up, the front wheels of the van lifted in the air and the trailer started to roll back. Thinking it may have been a matter of weight, Joe and I piled into the front seat along with Jill, and we also moved luggage up to the front. No matter how hard we tried or how much of a run we got, the van kept doing the same thing. The hotel maintenance man arrived, looking as though he were doing his best not to laugh. He hooked the trailer to his big SUV and pulled it easily up to the top.

After leaving Seattle, we took a ferry ride from Port Angeles, Washington, to Victoria, the provincial capital of British Columbia. Victoria was our first international destination. When we got our first passport stamps, I gave the kids a strict lecture about our rules for international travel: "No flying solo. We need to stay together as a group and watch each other's backs at all times. If we get separated, find a policeman and ask him to take you straight to the American Embassy."

Jill said, "Don't you think that's a little much? Shouldn't they just go wait by the ferry? It's in plain view, and we're only here for a day. Besides, the embassy is in Ottawa, two thousand miles away."

"You know what I mean—the embassy helper place . . . the consulate," I said. "There are a lot of perverts in Canada, and besides, I want the kids to have an emergency plan in place to practice for the really dangerous places we are going, like Turkey."

We survived Victoria and then moved on to Rexburg, Idaho, where Jill's parents were spending the summer. At the Fourth of July parade, Jill found a two-year-old who was separated from his mother. He stayed with us for an hour until his mother showed up. "See, just like I said, it can happen," I told Jill. "Kids get separated from their parents all the time."

With more than a hint of melodrama in her voice, Jill replied, "Instead of looking for his mom, do you think I should have just taken him to the American Embassy?"

In Rexburg we completed a lot of our international trip preparation. We finalized our itinerary for the first five months overseas and filled out paperwork to buy a car in Europe. With each of these steps, the international part of our trip became more and more of a reality. It was still possible to cancel, but now it would cost us a lot of money to do so.

It was hard for all of us to say goodbye to Grandma and Grandpa, as we would not see them for an entire year. Somehow when you say goodbye to older people, there is always the sense that the next time you see them they may be holding a lily while someone dressed in black is saying prayers in Latin over them. This concern was magnified by the fact that during parts of our travels it would take days to get back home.

We spent the next six weeks driving across the country. Our route included stops in Des Moines, Chicago, St. Louis, Indianapolis, Knoxville, and Cook's Forest in Pennsylvania. We were pleasantly surprised at how well the kids were getting along during long car rides. The constant bickering of the first few days was gone. They would still fight for about ten minutes when they first got in the van, and they would fight as we were pulling in to the next stop, but the time in the middle was peaceful as they slept, read, or watched DVDs, mostly leaving one another alone.

We also were surprised by how much they loved travel. Whenever we arrived somewhere new, the kids would immediately set out to explore. Most of the places we stayed were campgrounds that provided brochures for the activities nearby. Joey would return from the office with a handful of these brochures and plenty of ideas about what we could do. One day I asked Joey what he liked so much about being on the road. He said, "I like exploring the unknown, I like being on my toes."

We found that we got the most out of a place if we had read a little about it beforehand, especially about an area's history and culture. We also were interested in regional foods. One of our goals during our year of travel was to find the world's greatest pizza, and so in each new town we asked the locals where to find "the best pizza in town." We began a list of our favorites. As we drove through Tennessee, Cami asked, "What kind of special pizza does this place have?"

I said, "Well Cami, we are in the South, so I suspect they will have possum."

Cami replied, "Does that taste anything like unicorn?"

Many home-cooked meals are better than those purchased in a restaurant, but not pizza. To create a truly great pizza requires not only the best ingredients, but a dedicated pizza oven. Pizza should be just enough of everything without being too much of anything. I love cheese, but too much of it will ruin a pizza.

We ate lots of pizza. I wonder what family therapists would think if they were there to watch us order. This is how the conversation typically went:

Joe: I'll take a large pepperoni and mushroom.

David: I'll split it with you. I prefer thin crust.

Joe: I prefer thick.

David: I prefer thin.

Joe: Can we at least get an order of cheese bread for an appetizer?

David: That's redundant, because pizza is essentially flattened cheese bread with sauce and toppings. Besides, that's expensive. Do I look like a bank?

Jill: Cami and I will split a cheese pizza.

Cami: Do we have to have pizza? I don't like pizza. I want chicken nuggets. And can we just this once get dessert?

Tommy: Dad, could we please put mushrooms on only half the pizza?

David: Sure, buddy.

(Waiter arrives at the table.)

David: Do you have any specials? Are there any service charges? Is tap water free?

Joe, Tommy, Cami (all together): Can we just this once have Sprite?

On the surface, this discussion is about pizza—but it's really about how we make decisions as a family. In other words, this discussion is about values and power.

Joe wants to get his way. Tommy wants to get along. Jill wants to take care of Cami. Cami wants to know that we love her enough to order her something special. I want to show "the prince" that I am still king, to acknowledge and encourage Tommy's selfless behavior, and (of course) to conserve the trip money.

One day, we all went to the University of Tennessee's track and field stadium to see our cousin Matthew high jump. It was crowded and steaming hot, and we were the only white folk in our section. The high jump pit was on the other side of the stadium, and we began making our way up the jam-packed stairway to the exit with Jill in front and the kids and I about fifteen steps behind. The kids were in full bellyaching mode, complaining about the heat and humidity.

Jill turned, cupped her hands over her mouth, and yelled, "Be quiet guys! This is exactly what Africa is going to be like!" She was referring to the weather, but the African-Americans who crowded the stands looked at her and shook their heads.

Our biggest problem had to do with food—specifically, snacks. Before we left home, the kids cleaned out their savings accounts (they had roughly $250 apiece) and put all the money onto a Visa gift card. We allowed them to spend it however they wished.

Whenever we stopped for fuel, the kids would hurry into the filling station convenience store, study each item in the snack aisle, and head for the cash register, where they pulled out their gift cards.

Back in the van, they feasted on Pringles, ice cream, or "flaming hot" Cheetos. Not surprisingly, they never purchased anything healthy like fruit or yogurt. We figured they would tire of this after a few days, but it only seemed to get worse. One day, Tommy picked out a huge bag of Bugles, Joey was contemplating a Moon Pie, and Cami had graduated to the quart size of Ben and Jerry's.

We had to do something. First, we tried logic: "If you spend all your money at the Quickie Mart here in South Dakota, you won't have any money left to buy souvenirs when we get to Africa." Surely they would understand the importance of delayed gratification. This sound rhetoric was met by blank looks.

Being Catholic, we tried guilt. "You are spending money given to you on Jesus' birthday. He died for your sins, and I don't think he would want you to be buying junk food. Furthermore, there are people starving all over the world while you are overeating." More blank looks.

Then Jill and I came up with the idea of a "dollar snack." The kids could each have one snack per day as long as it cost under a dollar and had less than three hundred calories. Furthermore, we would pay. If one of them didn't want a snack, we would give that child the dollar to save or to spend on some other non-food item. Having solved this problem in such a wise and just manner, we congratulated each other on our sublime parenting and slept the sleep of the innocent that night.

We implemented the dollar snack system the next day.

"What about tax?" Joey asked.

"Huh?" I replied.

"Well, these cream-filled raspberry Zingers are a dollar, but tax will bring them up to $1.06."

Jill said, "Sure, no problem."

I disagreed. "It's a dollar total." Joey shook his head and picked out a candy bar instead.

Then Tommy walked up with a big bag. "These pork rinds are over three hundred calories. They are actually seven hundred," he said. "So can I eat two-fifths today, two-fifths tomorrow, and one-fifth the next day, and then take my dollar for the next two days?"

Jill, who was soon to begin teaching math to Tommy, said, "Sure, no problem. By the way, good use of fractions!"

I said, "Wait a minute. That's a violation of the spirit in which the rules were made." Tommy stomped off to join Joey in the van.

Later in the trip, "buy one, get one free" Skittles created a huge controversy. "We are only spending a dollar, and we get two big bags of Skittles! Why can't we buy one, get one free, and eat them both?" queried the kids.

"Because you would be getting way more than three hundred calories."

"Why can't we eat one today and save the other one for tomorrow and then save tomorrow's dollar?"

The kids learned to pick food with marginal nutritional value and then ask if the treat counted as a dollar snack. One day, while Cami was hugging me and pleading with her big blue eyes, she contended that chocolate milk shouldn't count for a dollar snack because it has lots of protein and it's good for you. I'm proud to say I didn't fall for this manipulation. Cami returned the chocolate milk to the refrigerator. Then she picked out a big candy bar that had no calorie content listed.

Jill and I did not want be an inconvenience to people we visited. We didn't want to be thought of as sponges. We decided that we would sleep in the trailer regardless of where we were. If people really wanted us to stay with them, we would park the trailer in their driveway, hook up to their water and power, and stay there.

But after a month on the road, the trailer was becoming uncomfortable. There are five of us, and the trailer was only nineteen feet long. Whenever someone got up to use the bathroom—especially Joe, who shook the trailer like a rhinoceros—the rest of us would wake up. We soon got over our concerns about being moochers, and we happily unhooked the trailer and stayed in the homes of family and friends.

Living in Arizona for most of the year and spending summers in Alaska, we frequently have had guests stay at our home, but it had been a while since we stayed with other people. Yet time and again, people we had not seen in years welcomed us into their homes.

As we would prepare to leave, the same people who had stopped their busy lives to cook for us and show us around would say, "Thank you for making us part of your trip." It seemed to us that our hosts, especially the older ones, sensed the importance of our trip more than we did. Being thanked always felt awkward. We were the guests, and we were the ones who should be saying "thank you."

The kindness shown to us was touching beyond words. We were taken to lunch, dinner, and out for ice cream. We were cooked for, cleaned up after, taken water skiing, golfing, and on numerous local tours. All that was terrific, but almost always the best part was sitting around visiting, taking the time to talk and get reacquainted.

The camper had an awning that rolled out to provide protection from the elements. Try as I might, I could never get it to go out straight or roll back up. One rainy day in Cook's Forest, Pennsylvania, Jill's cousin Al was helping me unroll the awning. Midway through he stopped, looked me right in the eye, and said, "Do you have any idea how many people there are sitting around in nursing homes who wish they would have done something like this when they had the chance?"

It was a question I will never forget. My answer (which I did not give) was, "No. It had not occurred to me." The significance of what we were doing was frequently lost in the day-to-day business of travel.

By now, the trailer was a mess, with garbage everywhere. The boys and I washed and waxed the outside and Jill worked for two days on the inside, making it spotless. We put an advertisement in the Burlington paper and then parked it near the Vermont State Fair with a "for sale" sign in the window.

After four days the only response we received was from some weirdo who said he did not want to buy it but would live in it for us until we came back. We drove down to pick it up and saw a woman standing outside of the trailer, writing down our phone number. She couldn't believe how clean the trailer was and she bought it the following day for our asking price, a mere two hundred dollars less than what we originally paid.

Before we left on this trip, people often would ask which place in the whole world I was most looking forward to seeing. I think they expected me to answer India or Africa. In all honesty, the place on earth I most wanted to see was the Baseball Hall of Fame in Cooperstown, New York. Cooperstown is a picturesque town in a rural area of northeastern New York. The closest big city is Albany. Cooperstown has a classic main street with tasteful shops and restaurants, but no go-kart tracks or mini golf. Lake Otsego is close by.

High expectations often beget disappointment, but the Baseball Hall of Fame was even better than I expected. The outside of the museum is as understated as the town itself. I arrived early, expecting large crowds, but saw only a few little leaguers with their coaches.

One of my favorite exhibits was a case that holds an autographed ball from every no-hit game that has been thrown since the 1950s. I had listened to or been at four of those games:

September 26, 1983—Bob Forsch (STL), 3–0 over the Montreal Expos. I was sitting in my 1969 Mustang outside the McDonalds by Saint Louis University.

August 28, 1991—Dennis Martinez (Montreal), perfect game 2–0 over the Dodgers. I was driving my mother-in-law's car back through Salt River Canyon as Vin Scully faded in and out on the radio.

June 25, 1999—Jose Jimenez (STL), 1–0 over Diamondbacks. Went to that one with Jill and no one in the Arizona crowd had a clue until the 9th inning.

May 18, 2004 Randy Johnson (AZ), perfect game 1–0 over Atlanta. Like a good dad, I was sitting in the parking lot outside my daughter's graduation recital from preschool—listening on the radio.

I explored the museum by myself for the two hours, and then returned in the afternoon with Joe and Tommy. The boys enjoyed the Hall of Fame, but not to the degree I did. I was giddy and needed to call someone who would understand. I called my friend Michael Bossone.

Michael is a passionate baseball fan who had been to the Hall of Fame as a boy. He listened eagerly as I told him about some of the newer exhibits. He then told me that his family owns the Squan Tavern restaurant on the New Jersey shore, only a few hours' drive from Cooperstown. Michael was convinced that his parents would love to have us as guests.

"Michael, that's very kind, but we have never met your parents," I said. "We don't want to be an inconvenience. How about if we stay in a nearby hotel and go by the restaurant?" Michael noted that his parents would be deeply insulted if we didn't stay with them.

"Besides," he added, "I doubt you will be able to find a hotel room on Labor Day weekend."

That night in a campground near Cooperstown, we met some Dutch kids who had never played baseball in their lives. I gave them some coaching on how to hit and threw some batting practice with them.

These Dutch youngsters knew about the Baseball Hall of Fame, and they asked if I was in it. That made me feel pretty good about myself, until Joey brought me back to reality. "Dad," he said, "your best fastball is thirty-five miles per hour, these kids can't name a single real big league baseball player, and they refer to baseball as 'honkball.'"

CHAPTER 4

PIZZA

Finding Old-World Culture Close to Home |

"I think staying with Michael's family is a bad idea," Jill said. "We see Michael once, maybe twice, a year and have never met his mom and dad. This isn't like crashing on your friend's couch when you are in college. There are five of us, David. These people run a restaurant. It's a holiday weekend, and I'm sure they are tired and have better things to do than entertain a bunch of moochers."

"Don't worry. It'll be fine." I replied. "This is a great chance for the kids to witness the inner workings of a family restaurant."

Jill had the upper hand in this discussion. From a moral standpoint, "It's wrong to inconvenience people" trumps "Free pizza!" With just a little pressure Jill could have had her way, but she backed off. "I honestly didn't feel right about staying with them," she later explained, "but I knew how much it meant to you."

We headed south to the New Jersey shore. Traffic was heavy and we arrived two hours late. Michael's mom, Marguerite Bossone, had been waiting for us at Squan Tavern, the family's restaurant. Dominic, Michael's dad, was at the track for the final horse race of the season. I ordered a pepperoni and mushroom pizza, and when it came, Mrs. Bossone joined us for lunch.

Cami asked, "So Dad, where is this pizza in the contest? Is it first?"

We explained the pizza contest to Mrs. Bossone. She looked at me inquiringly. I continued eating.

Cami persisted: "Dad, where is it on the list? Is it first?"

I tried diplomacy. "Well Cami, there are a lot of pizzas in the world and we haven't even left the country yet."

"I know Dad, but where is it so far?"

Asking Cami to be quiet would only have made things worse. It was in fact very good pizza; crisp thin crust, good pepperoni, just the right amount of sauce.

It would have ranked fourth. But could I say that?

This is printed on the cover of the Squan Tavern menu:

> *For all these years we have poured our hearts and souls into establishing the Squan Tavern as one of the premier Italian restaurants on the Jersey Shore. We have been through many changes over that time, but what has never changed is our commitment to providing our customers with Italian food that would make our ancestors proud.*

The pizza in front of me, which tasted like pepperoni and mushrooms, was actually *hearts and souls*—and in my pathetic contest, this pizza was not going to win, place, or show? On the other hand if the contest was going to have any credibility, I had to be honest. Mrs. Bossone was still looking at me. I stammered, "Well, uhhh . . . Cami, I need to think about it."

We weren't getting off on the right foot, and it was about to get worse. Mrs. Bossone drove the kids to the family home in her Lincoln Town Car while Jill and I followed in the minivan. Mrs. Bossone showed us to our room and then returned to the restaurant.

I opened a back door of the house and set off the burglar alarm. A few seconds later, the phone rang. It was the alarm company calling, and they wanted to know the alarm password. I guess "How the hell should I know?" was incorrect because within minutes, a police car pulled into the driveway.

I greeted the officer. "You aren't one of the Bossones," he said. I explained that we were visitors, and he asked me for identification. My wallet was in my pocket and I could have just pulled out my driver's license, but I now had a passport that I couldn't wait to show off, a passport with not one but two Canadian passport stamps. The police officer looked at the passport, looked at the Canadian stamps, and then looked at me. Unimpressed, he asked for my driver's license. The officer wrote down the number on his police report and then eyeballed me one last time before driving off.

That evening, we returned to Squan Tavern for dinner to find patrons lined up through the bar and spilling out onto the sidewalk. Michael's sister led us into the restaurant where every table was full—except the one waiting for us. Mr. and Mrs. Bossone joined us for dinner.

Joe ordered spaghetti and meatballs. The meatballs were incredible—baked not fried, with a firm texture and subtle spices, just the right amount of garlic. No bill was presented, and when I reached for my wallet I got the "don't even think about it" look from Mr. Bossone.

In Italy, life revolves around family, and family revolves around food. Owning a restaurant is a prestigious occupation in Italy, and choosing to have dinner at a restaurant is a personal compliment to the restaurant owner. That owner responds by treating you as thought you are a guest in his home. Observing him as he made the rounds greeting many of the guests by name, it was clear that Mr. Bossone carried this tradition from Italy to New Jersey.

I watched the unhurried way the waitresses interacted with the customers and noticed a bounce in their step that hard-working folks at the end of a week frequently lack. This was not the phony "have a nice day" pseudo-perkiness of someone hoping for a tip, rather it was the look of someone gratified with their work. I wondered how many times they had been asked to take a photo for a birthday or anniversary. I wondered how many wedding proposals they had witnessed? I wondered how many sentences now begin with the words: "Remember that night at Squan Tavern when. . . ."

The restaurant was closed on Labor Day, but Mr. Bossone opened it to teach us how to make pizza. Joe made meatball and mushroom. While everyone else in town was spending the final day of summer at the beach, we ate pizza outside in the shade on a gorgeous afternoon. The thinly sliced meatballs were a perfect topping, so much so that the Squan Tavern pizza was now a legitimate second place in the pizza contest.

The twenty-five hundred meatballs for the week are made every Tuesday at 6 a.m. We missed the early start, but the extended Bossone family, including aunts and cousins, welcomed us at 7:30 just in time to help make (and eat) some of the final batches.

Being welcomed inside another culture is what every traveler dreams of in large measure because it is so rare. When we planned this trip, I envisioned us as cultural insiders in Zanzibar or Patagonia. Yet here we were still in the United States—in *New Jersey* of all places—and the experience of the last few days was a genuine immersion into another culture. Our entire family was grateful.

Michael's sister took us for one final walk on the now-deserted beach. I told the kids that the next time we would see the Atlantic Ocean, we would be on its eastern shore in Normandy, France. We packed up at noon and headed for Trenton.

It was another beautiful day, and as we pulled onto northbound Interstate 95 some papers flew off the dashboard. Jill picked them up and tucked them between my belt and the role of flab above it. "That ought to hold them," she said patting my belly. "Those meatballs are like paperweights."

We dropped our van at an auction place in Trenton, New Jersey, and after a quick taxi ride, we boarded the train for New York City. There, we connected with the NYC subway in Penn Station. We had heavy wheeled luggage and were pleased with the calm way the kids maneuvered through Penn Station and onto the Green Line north to 77th Street. We exited the subway and lugged our heavy suitcases up the steps, out the gate, and into bright September sunshine on the busy sidewalks of Manhattan.

Worried about becoming separated, Jill told the kids to pretend we were a family of ducks, and to walk single file with me in the front, the three kids behind, and Jill in the rear. This method failed because I walk slowly, lack a sense of direction, and am easily distracted. After a few days, a more natural pattern of walking emerged, with Joe in the lead, and Tommy by his side. Joe marched with a true sense of purpose, looking supremely confident—à la MacArthur wading ashore in the Philippines. Occasionally, Joe would go the wrong way, but even then he was never in doubt. Jill is the family navigator. She could always be found with a map in her pocket, holding Cami's hand, a short distance behind the boys. I was at the back. Every two blocks, Joe and Tom slowed to wait for Jill and Cami. Then the whole family would have to wait for me.

Our kids loved New York. The energy that they noticed when we first walked out of the subway stayed with them the entire week. We went to plays, a ballgame at Yankee Stadium, the Museum of Natural History, and the Metropol- itan Museum of Art. One drawback was that every attraction has a gift shop that you must pass through in order to exit. We dreaded these gift shops, especially now because we were trying to get rid of unessential items. We had long ago grown tired of fighting with the kids over souvenirs, so sometimes we would say, "We will give you a three-dollar reward if you can make it through the gift shop without buying anything."

In art museums, we handled matters differently. Our kids don't have much of an art background, and we weren't worried that they would want to spend money on the latest Matisse coffee table book. The threat in art museums was boredom. In order to combat this, we turned museum visits into treasure hunts. We started in the gift shop. The kids would select a postcard of a work of art within the museum, and we would time how long it took to find it. Once they found the painting or sculpture, the kids had to give a brief presentation about that work of art. No two objects could be in the same section, which guaranteed that we would walk by a lot of different stuff.

At the Metropolitan Museum of Art, Cami picked a card showing an an- cient Egyptian wood carving of a deer. We looked and looked for that deer, and it took over an hour to find because it was tiny, only about three inches tall. Joe picked the famous painting of Washington crossing the Delaware, and Tommy chose a card with a suit of armor. We never did find that, because it was out on loan to another museum. Were it not for Joe, our scheme would have failed. Unlike most thirteen-year-olds, he loved museums. Furthermore, once we were inside, Joe never forced us to leave early. Cami and Tommy followed the lead of their big brother. If he was happy to stay, they also stayed without complaining.

We had been advised to get our travel visas ahead of time. One muggy morning, I walked to the Indian consulate on E. 64th Street. The visa office was down some outside concrete steps and even though I arrived half an hour before it was due to open, there was already a crowd of people standing around to enter the packed, dirty room. There were no lines, just a mass of people. A process that took two hours when we obtained our Tanzanian visas took all day here, and when I finally arrived at the front of the line, the clerk explained from behind a glass teller window that since we live in Arizona, I would have to pay an additional fee and fill out additional papers. Sensing she wanted a little *baksheesh*, I put fifty dollars in the tray, looked at her, raised my eyebrows, then casually turned my head away. This was my first attempt at bribery, and it failed. When I turned back, President Grant was right where I had left him, and the clerk was looking at me and shaking her head.

Tension began to build as we made last-minute preparations to leave the country. We called our credit card companies and banks to give them detailed information about our travel plans. We called friends and family one last time, ate hamburgers and deli sandwiches, winnowed our possessions to the international weight limit of twenty kilograms per suitcase, and donated what was left.

The night of September 11, 2007—six years since the World Trade Center attacks—was our last in the United States. After dinner we took a subway to the Brooklyn Heights promenade, a beautiful spot that provides a postcard view of lower Manhattan. On the land where the World Trade Center had stood, twin beams of light rose up, penetrating through the clouds before disappearing into the night sky, symbols to the world that America remains undaunted.

Standing there looking back across the East River, I was very much daunted. Those beams are a symbol of our resilience but also a reminder that not everyone likes Americans. The last three months had been great. We had traveled across the country harmoniously and under budget, feted by friends old and new. We had enjoyed a grand vacation on our home turf. Tomorrow we would leave all that behind and take our precious children into the big, violent, anti-American world.

When you have done your best you should await the result in peace. We had done our best to prepare for this trip, but at that moment, it didn't seem nearly enough. Standing on the promenade I looked at Jill, shook my head, and said, "I don't know about all this."

She smiled and said, "Don't worry. We'll be fine."

CHAPTER 5

AFRICA

Balance in the Serengeti | *September 22–October 6, 2007*

*E*ngland was an expensive ten-day sojourn. A McDonald's meal that would cost our family nineteen dollars in New York cost us forty dollars in London. Hotels also were very expensive. In York, we checked into a nice hotel and were informed by the staff that we were expected to "dress for breakfast." The following morning, since none of us had fancy clothes, they seated us near the kitchen, from which arose a rotting odor. The source of this stench was black pudding, a British dietary staple made by cooking blood with filler until it is thick enough to congeal. "One hundred dollars to whoever takes a bite," I said looking at the boys, knowing Jill and Cami would never consider it.

"No way," Joe said.

"Me either," said Tommy.

"OK, fine," I replied. "The offer remains good for the entire trip. One hundred dollars to whoever eats the most disgusting thing."

We enjoyed our time in England. We had successfully adjusted to the time change and had begun to settle in regarding international travel. But as we waited for our flight from Heathrow to Nairobi, our anxiety was building. We had called Kenya Airlines the day before to confirm our reservations. They informed us that we were confirmed from London to Nairobi, but there had been a mix-up on our flight from Nairobi to Arusha, Tanzania, and we would now have to fly standby.

Normally, this would be a minor inconvenience, but we paid in full for our safari and any missing days would be non-refundable. Adding to our trepidation was the possibility of having to spend the night in Nairobi, an allegedly dangerous city. We received some good news upon check-in at Heathrow. Kenya Airlines said everything had been worked out and our bags had been checked through to Arusha. However, if for some reason we missed our connection, it was back to standby status.

When we made the decision to visit Africa, Botswana—not Tanzania—was our first choice. We have always loved the film *The Gods Must Be Crazy*, and the more we learned about the Okavango Delta, the more incredible it seemed. But even budget safaris in Botswana were too expensive. We chose Tanzania for its safety, cost, and abundant wildlife.

Virtually every country in Africa was at one time a colony, and the countries carry forth characteristics of their colonizers. Tanganyika was initially colonized by the Germans. After World War I, the British made it a protectorate of sorts. Tanganyika achieved its independence in 1961, and then merged with Zanzibar in 1964 to create the new country we now know as Tanzania.

Except for a few bumps at the beginning, The United Republic of Tanzania has been remarkably free of the usual African problems with tribalism and corrupt dictators. Some of the credit for this goes to the father of Tanzania, Julius Nyerere. When he came to power, more than 120 languages were spoken in Tanzania, and most tribes didn't understand each other. Shortly after his election in 1961, Nyerere made Swahili the country's official language. This facilitated better communication and more intermarriage among tribes, which decreased the likelihood of conflict. Nyerere attempted to make Tanzania a socialist and self-supporting state, and in this regard he failed. Tanzania remains a desperately poor country with a per capita GDP of only one hundred dollars per month.

While the country is new, civilization in Tanzania is ancient. Known as the "cradle of mankind," northern Tanzania is home to the world's oldest known human settlement, and archaeologist Mary Leakey unearthed the two million-year-old fossilized bones of a four-foot-tall, small-brained biped known as *Paranthropus boisei* within the country's borders.

When I booked our around-the-world tickets and noticed we would be flying Kenya Airlines, I expected the in-flight meal to be goat cooked over a charcoal fire, served by a stewardess with a bone through her nose. While waiting for the flight, I prepared the family for the worst. Kenya Airlines turned out to be quite nice, with delicious food and a state-of-the-art entertainment system. We arrived in "Nai Robbery" at 6 p.m., exactly the time our connecting flight was supposed to depart. To my immense relief, our connecting flight was also delayed and was now due to leave at 9 p.m.

After carefully searching our bags, the Nairobi airport security staff ushered us into a departure lounge to wait for the flight. Our Plexiglas-enclosed "lounge" had thirty yellow plastic chairs to accommodate well over one hundred passengers waiting for four different flights. The floor was too dirty to sit on, so we stood. Some passengers who arrived in the lounge an hour after us were leaving before us. When the kids had to go to the restroom, I watched the expressions on their faces as they saw their first-ever squat toilet.

By midnight, we had assumed control of four of the precious yellow seats. Cami was asleep on my lap. Assuming that our flight was canceled, I wondered whether we should spend the night in the uncomfortable but safe departure lounge or look for a hotel. Some of the Kenyans who were waiting for the same flight we were became impatient and began shouting at the ground crew. This seemed to provide them with a new sense of urgency, and they made an announcement that an aircraft would be available soon.

An hour later, a twin-engine turbo prop pulled up. We were hurried onto the tarmac and told to ignore our seat assignments and sit in any open seat. Cami and Jill sat together, but the rest of us were spread out. I felt relieved. The logistics we had gone to such lengths to put in place would stay in place, we wouldn't have to spend a night in Nairobi, lose money on our safari, or rebook our aircraft. Within minutes we were in the air and bound for Arusha.

Africa boasts nearly a billion people, accounting for over one-sixth of the world's population, but the continent generates only 4 percent of the world's electricity. As I looked out the aircraft's window the ground appeared to be in total darkness. When we arrived in Arusha at 2 a.m., Eddie, our safari guide, was waiting for us. We reached the hotel, and the front desk clerk said, "Because of your lateness we have given your rooms away, but *hakuna matada*, you will now have lucky sleep in the ambassador's residence." The "ambassador's residence" turned out to be a lovely three-bedroom house with its own private garden, a flagpole in the driveway, and a small cannon, presumably to be fired whenever an ambassador was ready to start the day. Too tired to appreciate this lovely place, we fell into our beds at 3 a.m., and slept until 6, at which time we left for our pre-safari briefing.

One of my biggest worries about our safari was being grouped with other people. I have been on long outdoor trips with obnoxious people, and it made for a bad experience. Now that we had kids, I worried even more. What if our fellow travelers didn't like kids or didn't like Americans? Worse yet, what if they were bird watchers? I know a few bird watchers, and they are nice people, but they also are relentless when it comes to adding to their life list. Tanzania has some of the best bird life on Earth, and I could just imagine how bored the kids would be if instead of watching elephants we spent all day searching for a kori bustard.

To my great relief, we discovered that no one else would be joining us. We were to have a private safari. At our pre-trip meeting, we had been asked what our goals were. We said: "See a lot of critters" and "don't get eaten by any of them." While double-checking our medical evacuation insurance and having us sign the liability release, Eddie laughed and told us that we probably wouldn't get eaten. He then reminded us that we had chosen a budget safari, which meant we would be sleeping in old canvas tents in unfenced campgrounds. If we were really worried about being eaten, he said, we could pay more money and change to a lodge safari. I looked at Jill. "Tents," she said, while nodding her head. I agreed.

We loaded our bags into a Toyota Land Cruiser specially outfitted with four rows of seats and a rhino guard. On our way out of Arusha, we bought thirty-five candy bars and put them in a plastic cooler with no ice—one dollar snack per person, per day.

Over 28 percent of Tanzania is either a game reserve, national park, or conservation area. Game reserves still allow hunting and are generally associated with Teddy Roosevelt/Elmer Fudd safaris where the staff refers to you as *bwana* and you spend your days tracking and blasting critters followed by a smiling photo next to the carcasses, although most people who go to game reserves these days watch the animals instead of hunting them. We considered traveling to the Rufiji River in Selous Game Reserve. But, as with Botswana, getting there was difficult and expensive.

We chose instead a safari right on the beaten path of Tanzania's most well-known national parks—Serengeti, Lake Manyara, and the Ngorongoro Crater—connected by a 77-km paved road (a rarity in Africa). Choosing the easier, more commercial option gave me pause as a traveler, but because of the easier logistics, we could travel with well-rested kids and, as Jill said, "I'm sure these parks are famous for a reason."

It was mid-afternoon by the time we left Arusha, and we drove straight to Lake Manyara National Park to begin our first game drive. Eddie stopped the Land Cruiser, elevated the canopy-style roof, and we drove slowly down a bumpy dirt road. The first animal we saw was an impala.

Eddie explained that female impala herd together in large groups and rely on one male to protect them—and impregnate them. This male is constantly challenged by other male impala who are trying to take his job. The responsibilities of mating and protecting soon fatigues the male impala, and most manage to hold out for four weeks. Then another male takes his place.

Eddie described the impala as "a herd," but the impala weren't standing in a herd. They were grazing in a huge circle, as if drawn by a compass one might use in high school geometry class, with each one of them equidistant from the center point.

"Why are they standing in a big circle?" Tommy asked Eddie.

"Look in the grass in the center," Eddie replied. We looked with our binoculars but still didn't see anything. We waited. The impala farthest from us casually moved a few feet, distorting the circle. We looked above the grass again and briefly saw the heads of two cheetahs before they lay back down.

"Male cheetahs hunt in pairs," Eddie said. He then went on to explain that for the cheetah to have a chance to catch the impala it must sneak undetected to within the impala's "flight distance." That's another way of saying "head start." The cheetah has a chance if the race qualifies as a sprint and the head start the impala gets is less than one hundred yards; but if the race is longer, the impala wins every time. Older, younger, or injured impala will have a longer flight distance and will be easier for the cheetah to catch.

I had seen impala in zoos and never given them much thought. The cheetah changed everything. The peacefully grazing impala, instinctively understanding flight distance, could soon be racing for its life, and with just one slip, turn into a bloody meal. This drama—which will never be reproduced in zoos—captivated our entire family right from the start. I found myself conflicted: On the one hand, I wanted to see a bloody fight to the death, but I knew how much this would upset Cami. She just liked looking at the animals, especially the babies.

Farther down the bumpy dirt road, we saw a group of mongoose busily moving about a dirt mound, curiously popping their heads up and down. Eddie explained that mongoose dig burrows out in the open and far from shade. Many of the mongoose's predators are birds, and when the mongoose spots a shadow across its nest, it runs for the nearest hole.

Eddie had stories about so many animals, stories of animal behavior that thankfully omitted anthropomorphism. He was a wonderful guide who spoke fluent English and took the time to teach us a little Swahili. When we had spent enough time watching one animal, we simply said, "*Twende*" (Swahili for "let's go"), and he drove off to look for something else. At one point, Eddie pointed to an ostrich and said, "There are five families of flightless birds in the world. You have just seen one of them. Can any of you name another?"

"Penguins," Tommy and Cami shouted in unison.

"Emu," said Joe.

Jill mentioned the kiwi, but we couldn't come up with the final bird. Eddie told us about the nandu, which is found in southern South America.

On our way out of Lake Manyara, Eddie brought the Land Cruiser to a halt—a troop of about forty baboons were spread across the road. Many were in pairs, picking nits out of each other's hair, entirely oblivious to us. They sat there for a quarter of an hour and then slowly began moving across the road. One of the bigger males seemed to be acting like an evil simian crossing guard, standing in the middle of the road and pushing the baby baboons down or throwing them out of the way as they tried to cross.

Instead of camping in the park, we pitched our tent on its outskirts behind a corrugated metal fence in the middle of a terribly poor small town. A dirt road ran down the middle and occasionally a car would drive by, covering our tents in dust. After dinner, Eddie leaned against the hood of his safari vehicle and read his Bible. I waited for him to finish and then approached him to complain that this was too urban and too noisy. I informed him that we are an outdoor family and have spent many nights in Alaska bear country. We wanted to be out on the savanna, not in a town. Eddie said that it was the best he could do for now, but not to worry, as we would soon be in the wilderness.

Our campground provided protection from Cape buffalo and lions but not from Africa's most dangerous creature, the female anopheles mosquito. *Plasmodium falciparum malariais* is responsible for nearly a million deaths per year, most of them in children. We were prepared for the worst, with insect repellant, permethrine-treated clothes, special mosquito head nets and anti-malaria medicine that we had begun taking every day while we were still in England. To our surprise, there were very few insects. Eddie said this was because we were at the end of the dry season.

The next morning was Sunday, and as we ate our oatmeal breakfast, we heard lovely gospel singing coming from the half-finished building across the street. I told Eddie that if he wanted to join in worship we would go with him. We had not been to church since leaving the country, and this seemed like a great cultural experience. He explained that they were not his type of Christians and he didn't want to take part, so we drove off to hike in the Great Rift Valley.

The Great Rift Valley—visible from space—is an enormous seismic fault in the Earth's crust that stretches 3,700 miles from Syria in the north to Mozambique in the south. The minimum age for hiking here was fourteen, but we convinced them to make an exception. Cami did well with the hike, but she was wearing shorts and her legs were getting scraped up by thorn bushes, or "pokies" as Cami calls them. As we walked up the trail, a tall African man dressed in bright red clothes passed us. He was a Maasai tribesman on his way home. He picked up Cami and carried her through the "pokies." Then he walked us back to his village.

Maasai are polygamous. A typical village consists of a central house where the man lives and smaller houses for each of the wives and her children. The huts are placed in a circle around the pen where livestock are kept. This arrangement allows the Maasai to protect their cows and goats from being eaten by wild animals. The large igloo-shaped huts are constructed by placing cow dung mixed with straw over a frame of sticks. The cooking takes place inside but there is no chimney, so the houses get smoky. There is no electricity and no plumbing.

Maasai men are tremendous outdoorsmen. Traveling in pairs with little to drink, they herd cattle all day in the tropical sun. If food is scarce they will nick a cow's jugular vein with a knife and drink the blood. When they are away from home, Maasai sleep outside wrapped only in the blankets that they wear as cloaks during the day. If a lion decides it wants one of their cows, the Maasai have only their spears to dissuade the lion.

Maasai men are tough, but Maasai women are tougher still. The men herd the livestock; the women do everything else. Forced to undergo ritual circumcision at age nine (a practice that is now illegal but still occurs in secret), the women gather wood, collect water, take care of the children. They also build the houses. If there is a leaky roof, or if anything else goes wrong, the Maasai woman can expect a beating from her husband.

At the village a whole bunch of runny-nosed little kids came out to greet us. There was the usual hand gesturing between people who speak different languages. One five-year-old boy had caught a bird the size of a robin with his hands. Cami asked to see it, and the Maasai—assuming I guess that we were bird lovers—told the boy to let it go. He did as he was told, but he wasn't happy about it. Jill took pictures of the Maasai kids, and there was genuine amazement on their part when she showed them the digital images of themselves.

Two of the children went inside their huts and returned with leather necklaces. On each hung a discolored tooth that they insisted belonged to a lion. Tommy and Cami didn't buy the story—but they did buy the necklaces for a dollar. Joe took some Tanzanian shillings out of his pocket, shook his head at the necklace, and pointed to the Maasai's knife. After a few minutes of bargaining, Joe had purchased the knife and its red sheath for twelve dollars. The foot-long blade was well oiled, and the leather handle was stained with blood—a working-man's knife, not a souvenir. The Maasai assured us not to worry, that he could get another one.

The following morning, Eddie drove us to a different Maasai encounter. This one cost fifty dollars per person, paid for as part of our safari itinerary, and was billed as a "Maasai cultural experience." The Maasai are a people in transition, and the more business-oriented members of the tribe have come to realize that a culture of tall, exotic-looking nomads dressed in bright red cloaks is something people will pay to see.

When we arrived, a group of forty Maasai began humming and jumping up the way you would in a sack race minus the sack. The adults then gathered the kids and herded them into a phony classroom where the children recited the alphabet in English. It was clear that the letters written on the chalkboard had been there for months and were purely for our benefit. I guess the point was that by learning English they were bettering themselves, but how was that part of their culture?

The Maasai then showed us the souvenirs they had for sale and insisted we buy something. This was no native culture, but the bad side of tourism: planned, exploitative, and awkward. It would have been one thing if the culture or skill sets they demonstrated were legitimate, specifically if the cultural show included spear throwing, hut building, lion killing, or even turd collecting. But the "dance" show was of the quality I would expect from a five-year-old. Our kids saw through it too. "That was dumb," Tommy said. Eddie overheard him and smiled.

"*Serengeti*" is a Maasai word that means "endless plain," a vast, flat expanse of grasslands and trees, flat for as far as the eye can see. Admission to Serengeti National Park is U.S. $30 per person per day unless you are a Tanzanian citizen, in which case the fee is a dollar. Tommy didn't think this was fair. "If we charged Americans one dollar and foreigners thirty dollars to visit the Grand Canyon, no one would stand for it."

In Tanzania, safari guide is a prestigious occupation. We asked Eddie if he took advantage of this local discount to take his family out on safari. He smiled and said, "There is nothing I would like better than to take my children on safari, but even with the local discount, I could not possibly afford it."

Dirt roads wind through the Serengeti, and the relative absence of trees makes the savanna a great place for wildlife watching. Herbivores such as gazelles, zebras, and wildebeests are the most abundant animals, and the easiest to spot. Carnivores, such as the leopards and lions, are well camouflaged and more difficult to find, but they are there if you know where to look.

The sun was going down, and we were on our way to camp when Eddie hit the brakes and backed up. "*Simba*," he said, pointing to some rocks about fifty yards to the east of our vehicle. I have no idea how he spotted them, but hiding in a small crack there were four tiny lion cubs no bigger than house cats. We watched the cubs for ten minutes through our binoculars before they disappeared into the rocks. Their mother had left the cubs while she went away to hunt.

Lions are known as the "king of the jungle," but in Tanzania they don't live in the jungle, they live on the savanna, and the lioness actually does the hunting. According to Eddie, adult male lions are very powerful and good at protecting the pride, but bad at hunting. They are too slow to catch anything and their big furry manes make it difficult for them to sneak within the flight distance of potential prey, so they spend their days lounging around waiting for the females to bring home dinner.

Lions will kill any animal they catch and eat anything they kill except for hyenas, which they just leave for dead. According to Eddie, hyenas have jaws so powerful they can snap a cheetah's backbone. They are opportunistic animals who kill what they can but will also eat carrion.

Hyenas were abundant in the Serengeti, especially near sunset. They are easy to spot even in fading light because of their distinctive bear-like gait, which comes from having front legs that are longer than the back legs. Unlike most of the other animals, hyenas seemed to stare back as we stared at them.

That night we got the campsite I had hoped for. It was just after sunset when we arrived. As usual, our cook Damien was preparing dinner over a charcoal fire, but this time he was cooking inside a small rectangular hut with a mud brick foundation and a thatched roof. The cooking hut was framed with lumber and then wrapped in corrugated wire—much more formal than any of our previous campgrounds.

A large cinder block structure with a big water tank on its roof was fifty yards to the west across flat rocky ground. Eddie informed us that was the toilet. Jill, Cami, and I put on our headlamps and walked toward the bathroom. We were excited, because a water tank on the roof means running water inside. Whoever built this structure had good intentions but neglected to finish the job. Many of the cinderblocks were lying randomly about. A porcelain squat commode had been installed, but it was broken, as was the spigot—which, as expected, was dry. Outside the building, previous safari-goers had left a minefield of human feces. On our walk back to the dining room, while I prayed that none of our family came down with diarrhea, the beams of my headlamp illuminated a wooden sign nailed to a tree: "Caution! Do not get out of the campsite! Animal may attack human being." Atop the sign was a big animal skull complete with horns.

We had two small canvas tents. The boys and I were in one; Jill and Cami in the other. Eddie and Damien shared a tent between us. After dinner, Eddie turned to Jill and the kids, taking care to ignore me. "If you have to use the toilet, wake me and I will take you. And be sure to bring your shoes inside the tent because hyenas come into the campground at night and will steal them."

Lying atop my sleeping bag while watching the boys sleep soundly and hearing the patter of feet outside the tent, hearing the lions roar and the hyenas' too-frequent laughs, it dawned on me that we were fooling ourselves. An unfenced campsite is more a concept than a reality. Our canvas tents were zero protection against the powerful jaws of a hyena. All the tents did was compartmentalize things, offering us a false notion of a safe place when compared with the wildness outside. Still, that was enough to fool the kids and allow them to sleep soundly.

It may have fooled me too, but I couldn't get to sleep. I really had to pee. Jill had ordered special wide-mouthed water bottles so that she wouldn't have to leave the safety of her tent to urinate in the middle of the night. But that didn't help me. Normally I would have just stepped outside the tent and urinated, but I did not want to see a hyena in the moonlight. Even if there were no critters I feared a hyena might interpret the scent of my urine as a challenge to his territory. Furthermore, having complained about the urban campsite a few nights earlier and having boasted about my outdoorsmanship, waking Eddie was not an option. The sound of voices and the glow of the morning light finally solved my problem.

From the Serengeti we drove to the Ngorongoro Crater, a place with the highest concentration of wildlife anywhere on Earth. Midway through the first day we parked the Land Cruiser so Eddie could take a bathroom break. Jill and Cami were in the row behind Eddie, with Tommy and Joey in the middle I was in the rear bench seat by myself. A vervet monkey in a nearby tree took notice of us and sauntered over.

Cami said, "Oh, how cute! A monkey is coming to visit us."

I thought immediately of Curious George and turned around to look for the daypack, which held the camera. Using a soothing tone that works well with angry dogs, Jill began talking to the monkey. "Good monkey, nice monkey," she said. But this was *not* a nice monkey. He jumped through Eddie's open front window and into the car. "Get out of here, monkey!" Jill yelled. Instead of obeying, the monkey bared his teeth. Jill took the lid off the cooler and tried to push the monkey out of the car. When she did, the monkey stuck a hand inside the cooler and grabbed for the Snickers.

Jill pushed him back again this time as far as to the opening of the driver's window. I yelled for Cami to get out of the car. With the monkey pinned against the window frame, Jill quickly pulled the cooler lid back, then swung it hard, hitting in the monkey on the side of the head with enough force to knock him out of the car. Jill began frantically rolling the window up while the monkey turned back toward the car and screamed with rage. Eddie saw what was happening, picked up a couple rocks, and sprinted back to the car. The monkey caught sight of Eddie and ran quickly back to his tree.

"Did that monkey bother you?" Eddie asked.

"Yes," Jill said. "He tried to steal our chocolate. I'm glad you are here, because my husband was cowering in the back seat."

"I was looking for the camera," I said.

"I should have warned you." Eddie said. "They only bother white people. We throw rocks at them whenever they come close to us."

It was cold that night at our campsite at the top of the crater. We were drinking tea when someone came running in to tell us that an elephant was in the kitchen. We grabbed our flashlights and ran to see what was going on. As my manhood had been called into question earlier that day, I made the rest of the family wait behind me while I went forward to investigate. A huge bull elephant—bigger than any we had seen—had made his way into camp. He was in the kitchen, drinking from the trough in front of the water tank that the cooks use to prepare dinner. Bull elephants are some of the most dangerous animals on the planet, but this one was looking for water, not trouble. He leisurely drank until he had had enough, and then slowly walked away.

Our last stop on safari was another "cultural tour"; this one at a Ng'iresi village, a small agricultural town in the foothills of Mount Meru. The Ng'iresi were Maasai who had given up the nomadic life in favor of farming. Each family worked a small plot of land, but instead of growing just one crop at a time, they grew bananas and maize right next to each other. Custom dictated that when the father died, he divided his land equally among his sons. The result was that as each successive generation grew, the amount of tillable land they possessed shrunk.

We walked a mile with some of the Ng'iresi children to the stream where they fetch drinking water and then carry it back balanced on their heads. The little girl we accompanied was only four years old, and yet she was better at carrying the water than Joey, Tommy, or Cami.

The families here were desperately poor and many of the children looked malnourished. Jill and I hope to teach our children to be indifferent to most material things, but we felt obliged to point out that the Ng'iresi lacked the basics: clean running water, a private place to go to the bathroom, reliable shelter, and enough food to eat.

We tried to elicit a response from our children about how it felt to witness such poverty. We expected concern for the welfare of the Ng'iresi, anger at the injustice of it all, or even a clichéd, "Yeah, I sure feel lucky compared to them." But Joe, Tommy, and Cami were silent. Later, Joe spoke for all of them when he said, "I feel bad for how poor they are and all, but I think it's kind of cool that they get to get their water from the stream and they don't have any homework."

Our safari was over, and that night we returned to our initial hotel outside of Arusha. The ambassador's residence was occupied and we were put in standard hotel rooms, where we showered until all the hot water was gone.

While preparing for Africa we had frequently encountered the phrase "safari fatigue," a term that refers to boredom related to driving around bumpy, dusty roads looking for animals day after day. We expected the kids would get it, but they never did. It was a great family vacation in the truest sense of the word, meaning that all five of us loved it. Here are Cami's thoughts:

"You should go on a safari because it is really cool. If you look close enough you could see lions, giraffes and spotted hyena and lots more. My favorite animal was the baby lions. The biggest animal I saw was a elephant and a hippo. The smallest animal was the baby baboon." (October 2, 2007)

Eddie was waiting to drive us to the airport early the following morning. We were going to miss him. In addition to a well-deserved tip, we gave him our binoculars, two extra pairs of shoes, a pair of Joe's socks, and Jill's pee bottles.

Our next stop was the port city of Stone Town on Unguja Island, the largest in the Zanzibar archipelago. Stone Town was infamous as a slave-trading port. Arab slave traders rounded up men and women and brought them to Stone Town, where the Portuguese sold them as slaves and loaded them onto ships. That Arab influence was still very much on display as the whole city was fasting to observe the month of Ramadan. Ramadan is Islam's most holy month, a time when Muslims are required to abstain from both food and water from sunup until sundown each day.

After Tommy got a thirty-cent haircut, we set out to look for dollar snacks. It was hot and humid, and we were the only white faces in the crowded labyrinthine streets. Despite the crowds, the shops were all closed. A man approached us with a resounding "Hello."

"*Jambo*," I replied.

"Ah, I see you speak Swahili—very good. What are you searching for?"

"We are looking for a place to buy some snacks."

"It is Ramadan, so most of the shops are closed, but I know a place. Follow me."

We began to follow him, making turn after turn, and soon he was far ahead of us. We could still see him, but were becoming worried about finding our way back. Joe was particularly anxious, and we decided to turn back before we became helplessly lost. The man returned and caught up with us. "Why did you stop following me?" he asked.

"Well, we were feeling lost and quite frankly, we don't know you," I said.

"You could have at least caught up with me to tell me that," he said, while shaking his head and walking away.

"I'm sorry," I replied. And I genuinely was sorry. I felt guilty for wasting his time, but had we continued following him, I don't think we would have been able to find our way home, and he seemed a little too friendly.

We finally found a shop. The lights were out, but the people sitting near the window motioned for us to enter. They had a few warm Cokes and some Twix bars. Cami commenced to eat her candy bar on the way home and received more than a few angry looks from the fasting natives.

After three days, we hired a driver named Salim to take us on the thirty-mile trip from urban Stone Town to a beach resort on the northeastern part of the island. Salim spoke English in addition to Arabic, German, and Swahili. He was about ten years younger than I, and had three children the same ages as ours.

Salim was Muslim and he was fasting—no food, no drinks—all day in the Zanzibar heat. He said he didn't mind if we ate and drank if front of him. I asked if his children were fasting and he said they were, so out of respect Jill and I fasted that day and made our children do likewise. He explained that the dirty looks thrown Cami's way were because it is considered rude for even non-believers to eat in public during Ramadan. We were embarrassed to hear this. From the moment we left New York, we stressed to the kids that we were ambassadors of our country and as such should be respectful of other customs.

We drove along a dirt road, passing donkey carts that Salim referred to as "Tanzanian Ferraris." Tanzanian school kids all wear uniforms with blue shorts, white-collared shirts and sweaters, and whenever we drove by them, they waved to us and yelled, "*Pipi, pipi.* Good morning, teacher." Salim explained "*pipi*" is Swahili for "candy" and that the first English words the school kids learn are "Good morning teacher," so that was how they addressed all white people.

Ten miles outside of Stone Town, Tommy tapped me on the shoulder and whispered, "I have to drop a deuce." In Tommy-speak, that's "have a bowel movement."

"Salim," I said. "A toilet please—*Inshallah*" ("God willing").

"Yes, Mr. David, Inshallah," he replied as he immediately pulled the cab off the side of the road. Tommy looked questioningly at the roadside and then back at me. I shrugged and said, "Sorry buddy, I think this is the best place we are going to find." Tommy walked quickly to the side of the road to take care of his business.

The beach at the resort was flat and shallow—a mere three feet deep—for a half-mile, until reaching a sandbar where the waves broke. Joe, Tom, and I snorkeled toward the break in hopes of body surfing but turned back when we noticed the ocean floor was packed with spiky black sea urchins.

These three quiet days at a beach resort were planned as a rest stop to help us recover from "safari fatigue," but we didn't have "safari fatigue" and so we didn't feel like resting. We wanted to move. No matter how beautiful the place, it's hard to rest when you don't feel like it, and so we announced to the kids that the time had come to begin studying math.

We had refrained from formal schoolwork during our trip across the United States, but we promised them it would begin once we left the country. Because everyone was bored, this seemed like the perfect opportunity to start. To their credit, the kids didn't complain.

The hotel room was small and on the leeward side of the beach. The absence of wind made it hot during the day, so Joe took his math book and pencil to the hotel restaurant; a large open room with a constant cool breeze and a view of the beach—an idyllic place to graph inequalities. The only distraction was the cassette tape player blasting Barbra Streisand music. I looked around the restaurant and saw only a handful of other patrons, none of whom looked like Streisand fans. I asked the desk clerk to turn down the music. He checked with his boss and decreased the volume to a more tolerable level, but he didn't seem happy about doing so. One of the other guests caught my eye and mouthed the words "*asante sana*," which is Swahili for "thank you."

After two more boring days on staring at the Indian Ocean, we flew to Dubai. A word about arriving in countries by air: After landing, travelers are required to go through passport control, claim their bags, and then go through customs. Typically, the passport control agents perform their tasks with a bureaucratic indifference and a complete lack of urgency. Passenger comfort and traveler satisfaction are non-issues. Dubai was different. After landing, we walked down a well-marked hallway (Arabic, English, and French translations) to passport control where a polite, *dishdasha*-clad Arab welcomed us to his majesty's kingdom of Dubai and hoped we would enjoy our "all-too-brief visit."

As we waited for our luggage, we noticed an ad for the Burj Al Arab Hotel. The Burj Al Arab is designed to resemble a huge billowing sail and is billed as the world's only seven-star hotel. The ad assured us that the rate of $2,100 per night included not just our room but also a chauffeur-driven Rolls Royce ride from the airport and a brigade of highly trained butlers who would provide us with around-the-clock attention. The idea was tempting.

It struck me that the juxtaposition between rich and poor could never be better illustrated than by traveling from Zanzibar to the Burj Al Arab. Perhaps wretched excess could teach what poverty alone could not. The lesson may have been worth the cost, but we already had reservations for a three-bedroom apartment on the 25th floor of the Chelsea Suites at the "Ramadan special price of $225." We thought the 25th floor would be pretty high up, but our hotel was dwarfed by it's neighbor—the 1,680-foot Burj Dubai, the world's tallest building.

In Zanzibar, public eating during Ramadan was a social offense. In Dubai, it was criminal. Even non-believers were forbidden by law from eating or drinking in public, which was punishable by a fine or by imprisonment. In Zanzibar, I had not wanted to cause offense. In Dubai, I chafed at the tyranny, so whereas we had fasted by choice in Zanzibar, in Dubai we went to Burger King. When we arrived, the chairs were on top of the tables because no one was permitted to eat in the restaurant, though you could get food to go. We asked the cook if it was hard to fry burgers while fasting. He assured us that the burgers were flame-broiled, not fried, and said that it was very difficult the first few days of Ramadan but after that it became easier. I asked if he ever took a few French fries or perhaps a sip of Coke when no one was looking. He smiled. We ordered our combo meals and walked in 100-degree heat back to our apartment.

I want our children to appreciate other cultures, but I also want them to understand that this law was an affront to our liberty. I tried to get them to share in my outrage, but after two weeks of African food, the kids were busy enjoying their French fries, and all they wanted to talk about was our next stop, the Wild Wadi Water Park. The kids had visited the Wild Wadi website many times, enough to know the different waterslides by name, especially the Jumeirah Sceirah, which was billed as "the largest water slide outside of North America." The ad continued, "This 33-meter speed slide from which you will experience weightlessness as you travel at speeds up to 80 Km per hour."

As we waited in line for the Jumeirah Sceirah we overheard the woman in front of us speaking English. She was wearing an *abaya* (traditional Arab dress) and, assuming she was a local, we asked her about a building to the southwest of the water park with what looked like a big, bent aluminum can sticking out on its south side. She smiled and explained that that was the Dubai Emirates Mall and the metallic structure was the indoor ski hill.

Most of the water slides at Wild Wadi are for individuals—one person, one tube—but there was one slide designed for families. All five of us piled into a huge round rubber raft and prepared to be transported up a hill to begin our ride. The chamber in which we began was like the mother of all toilets, and as it filled with water it raised us up and then began to push us up a rubber ramp. Instead of continuing up, we slid back down. The toilet type mechanism tried to fill again but this time we didn't budge at all. A horn sounded loudly, a red light flashed, and the metal gate swung out over the rubber ramp. The ride shut down. One of the park employees who didn't speak a word of English emerged from behind a booth, pointed to my belly, and then shook his head.

To the great amusement of the kids, I got out and waited for the next raft. Sensing my embarrassment, Cami joined me.

We stayed at the water park until closing time. Afterwards, we visited the Mall of the Emirates, where Arab kids in traditional dress carried around snowboards. Joe and Tom said they wanted to ski but in reality they were both exhausted. The ski hill was tiny and we had to fly to France at 5 a.m. the following morning.

CHAPTER 6

EUROPE

Behind the Wheel | *October 8–November 14, 2007*

When we landed in Paris, Paul Azzara was waiting for us.

Paul was my high school French teacher and has remained a good friend ever since. On a previous trip to Europe in 1992, Jill and I met Paul in Arles, a small town in the south of France best known as the place where Vincent Van Gogh cut off his ear. Mr. Azzara, as we called him back then, proved to be such a knowledgeable and comfortable traveling companion that we asked him to join us for our two weeks in France.

Paul is now in his sixties, but you wouldn't know it. He is thinner and more fit than when I knew him in high school, although he still refers to himself as "short and bald." Our plan on this trip was to meet Paul in Paris, where a friend had generously offered us a free week in her apartment. Then we would drive to Normandy and finally the Loire Valley. Paul arranged all the details, which meant that Jill and I could take a break from travel planning and just enjoy the trip.

After a day of rest, which we spent reading *A Tale of Two Cities* aloud to the kids—we took the Metro to St. Chapelle, a beautiful old church with huge stained-glass windows. Afterward, Paul wanted to take us to Notre Dame, but instead we walked along the Seine looking for a bathroom for Tommy, whose intestinal system was still recovering from Tanzania. The next day, we visited Notre Dame, and the Louvre the day after that.

Here is what Tommy had to say in his journal:

The inside of Notre Dame was huge. It had a rose window. This Rose Window had pictures of the opacalipse. On the inside there were very many statues. One of the statues was of Saint Jonah Vark. She was a farm girl who led France to victory over Britan. She was later burned at the stake for witchcraft at 19 years of age. Jonah Vark was a great person.

The day after that we went to the Louvre. My brother, sister and I each got a statue or painting to talk about. Joey talked about the Mona Lisa. Cami talked about Venus de Milo, goddess of love, beauty and foolishness. I talked about Winged Victory. Winged Victory is a statue of Nike, goddess of victory. After the Louvre, we went to Place de Concord. That is a square where they would chop off people's heads using the geea tine.

We also went to Les Invalides, home of Napoleon's tomb and the French war museum. Paul informed us that Napoleon was believed to be buried *sans zizi* (without his penis), and that his shriveled up member was later purchased at auction by an American urologist. This rumor, while not found in the official museum guide, was hysterically funny to boys ages thirteen and nine.

At the top of the Arc de Triomphe, Tommy stuck his head between the metal safety railing bars and turned to look down the Champs-Élysées. A French security guard walked over, hit the railing with his baton, and said something to Tommy. This startled Tommy and he pulled his head straight back, but it wouldn't fit through the bars. With a smile on his face and allegedly "trying to help" Joe grabbed Tommy's forehead and pulled harder. Tommy's eyes filled with tears as the base of his skull wedged between the bars. We finally managed to free Tommy by having him stick his head out as far as possible then turn slightly to the left allowing his right ear to fit through the bar.

More family drama ensued. Here is Tommy's side of the story:

We went to the top of the Arc De Triomphe. the view was great. The Eiffel looked really great from up there. My little sister Cami kept kicking me even when I told her to stop, so I punched her in the face and gave her bloody nose. I almost forgot to say there are 284 stairs to the top of the Arc de triomphe.

This was business as usual for our family and wouldn't bear mentioning except we wanted the kids to be on their best behavior in front of Paul. He was fine with these shenanigans but was surprised by the slow pace of our trip. Paul was accustomed to leading large groups of high school students around Europe, where the goal is to see as many sights as possible during the day so they don't have the energy to get into trouble at night.

"Know thyself" is written above the Oracle at Delphi, and since we are for-ever evolving, we should forever revisit this maxim. In travel terms this meant Jill and I were constantly tinkering with the pace for our journey, searching for the right one. Most days, our pace was a compromise between Joe and Cami. Joe was relentless, always moving the trip forward, energizing us when we were tired. He could never see or do enough. Cami didn't complain when we went to museums or churches, but given the choice, she liked to sleep in and read Junie B. Jones books. She was only seven, after all.

On previous vacations, Jill and I (me more than Jill) would experience a creeping sense of guilt if we took a day off from sightseeing. Now, for the first time ever as travelers we were blessed with the luxury of time, a whole year. As the trip progressed we became more aware of this blessing and the freedom that accompanied it. We no longer felt remorseful if we took off a day, and we no longer felt obligated to visit every major attraction. We came to the realization that even if we had the rest of eternity we could never "see it all," and we were at peace with that.

As we would be spending the next six weeks driving in France and Italy, we purchased a nine-passenger Renault Expert Tepee van. "Purchasing" as opposed to renting was a dodge around the Value Added Tax, or VAT. Since we were not from Europe we were not required to pay the VAT when purchasing a car, and since the VAT did not apply to used cars, when we returned the car at the Renault dealer in Rome, it would be more attractive to a prospective buyer. We were required to buy the van before leaving the United States, which entailed filling out lots of paperwork and wiring money to an American intermediary. It was worth the hassle because the purchase saved three thousand dollars when compared to a conventional rental.

I read a survey once that said 80 percent of people consider themselves above-average drivers. I do not. I am most definitely a below-average driver. I can't parallel park, and I am often indecisive about when to turn. With great trepida-tion, I decided to drive in Europe anyway. Driving from the airport back to the apartment in Paris's 17th Arrondissement was easy. The roads were wide and well marked, and the drivers were polite. Paul and I picked up the rest of the family and began our journey to Normandy. The toll roads in France were nice, but quite expensive. Sometimes a day's driving would cost sixty Euros (eighty-seven dollars).

Paul had carefully printed out maps for our journeys from Paris to Norman-dy and then on to the Loire Valley. We wound up not needing the maps, because in Paris we bought a Global Positioning Satellite Navigation System. ("GPS" if you are in the United States, "sat nav" anywhere else). The GPS tells you exactly where you are, what direction you are traveling, and how fast you are approaching your destination. Ours was made by a company called Tom Tom and came loaded with maps of Europe and a list of voices to choose from. The voice Jill selected was named Tim. He spoke in a full-throated English idiom that seemed to say: "You may not know where you are, but I certainly do." Lord Nelson addressing his men could not have sounded more confident.

Tim was a polyglot capable of giving instructions in French, Italian, or German, and he could give those instructions in the metric or English system. He even beeped when a speed camera was approaching. We had driven throughout England with standard maps, and it was fine—but Tim was better, especially now that we were navigating on roads with French names.

Reliability was his only problem. Sometimes, Tim would quit speaking for extended periods of time and forget to tell us to turn. In cities his directions tended to lag. He might say, "Right turn in fifty meters" when we were in the left lane of a cramped four-lane road. Still, Tim smoothly navigated us to the farmhouse in Normandy where Paul had arranged for us to stay. It was a dairy farm with plenty of cats and dogs and even a few rats. When we arrived, the owner was surprised that we were American. Paul's French was so perfect that she was expecting a French family.

We toured the landing beaches at Normandy and then visited Pointe du Hoc, where American Army Rangers scaled a cliff to disable dug-in German soldiers. Pointe du Hoc was cratered from all the shelling and the kids crawled through German pillboxes, many of which were still intact.

If there is such a thing as a beautiful cemetery, it is the Normandy American cemetery that overlooks Omaha Beach and the English Channel. The cemetery is considered part of America even though it is located on French soil, and it is staffed by U.S. military personnel. As a way of saying thanks, the French gave America the land.

At the cemetery, we saw an elderly American man wearing a Veterans of Foreign Wars hat holding a folded flag. He was standing on some steps surrounded by a group of about fifteen people. He was beaming with emotion as he related a story, and though his eyes were dry, his audience was weeping. I assumed he had returned here with his friends and family to tell them about his experiences. Just seeing him made the battlefields and cemeteries much more personal, and soon we were crying too.

The following morning we went to Mass in the nearby town of Isigny. To our surprise, Mass was said in both French and German to accommodate a visiting group from Isigny's sister city, Weilerbach, Germany. Many of the churchgoers looked to be of World War II vintage, and afterwards we pointed out to the kids that it is possible for enemies to become friends.

Tim navigated us to our next stop, the Loire Valley, made all the more beautiful by the cool days and the colorful autumn leaves. We visited several castles, including Chenonceau, Chateau d'Amboise, and Chambord. The latter boasts 440 rooms and 365 fireplaces, and was built by King François I. Begun in 1519 and financed using tax revenues collected from peasants, Chambord took twenty years to build. Since the castle was not near a village or farm, there was no dependable supply of food, which limited its use. François rarely stayed at Chambord but showed it off as a sign of wealth and power to his rival, Emperor Charles V of Spain.

We were sad when we dropped Paul off at the Paris airport. None of the places we went were new for him, but true to his nature as a teacher he was excited to explain everything about each stop to our family.

It was back to the five of us, or six if you count Tim. He continued to say squirrelly things. In the middle of the Swiss Alps, Tim said, "Turn left, now get on the ferry." There was no water to be found, much less a ferry! The "ferry" turned out to be a train that took us through the mountains from Switzerland into Italy.

I was beginning to feel dependent on Tim. We no longer bought detailed maps or paid close attention to where we were going. For his part, Tim was feeling more and more in command of things. I could hear it in his voice, a voice that Jill seemed to find sexy. She has always loved British accents. Even when we weren't in need of directions, Jill would press the "voice check" button just to hear Tim speak.

Once we were in Italy, we spent a wonderful week visiting my cousins in Inveruno, a small town near Milan. My cousins had met Jill and me once before but had never met our children. They had presents waiting for each of us. We saw the house where my grandmother was born, and we met my newest cousin, Elisa, a two-year-old who dressed impeccably, drank tea, and ate mayonnaise straight out of the jar. She kissed everyone in our family except Tommy. Whenever he approached, she either looked away or shook her head.

I had heard that driving in Italy was not for the faint of heart, but the first week was okay apart from one little incident. We were staying in a campground near my relatives, and I needed to use the Internet. The town was small, and there were no Internet cafes, so I put on my best clothes, found a nice hotel, and sat in the lobby to use the free Internet intended for their guests. On the way back to the campground, I inched out into the intersection to make a left turn. Then I changed my mind, and backed up—crashing into a tiny blue Fiat. No damage was done to our monster van but I knocked the bumper off the Fiat and shattered its headlight. Had the same thing happened to me, I would have been furious, but the driver—a woman in her twenties with a newborn baby—was very understanding. In my broken Italian I apologized profusely and completely admitted fault. We filled out some papers, and I mailed them to my insurance company.

We left northern Italy the following day. As we approached Rome, the rules of the road began to change. The white lines painted on the road became purely decorative, and driving on the shoulder or the sidewalk became acceptable. Italy has three basic types of drivers. The first type likes to pretend they are Formula One drivers, in the same way that four-year-olds pretend they are Batman. Before leaving the house, these drivers put on their costume—leather driving gloves, sunglasses, and a little hat—and then they drive their Fiats as fast as they will go (typically topping out at eighty-five miles per hour) down the *Autostrade* in the left lane. They flash their lights at you to let you know that they are serious drivers (much more serious than you could ever be), so you had better move over. As they pass, they lean the car into you to show that they are the dominant male. (If they were dogs, this is when they would pee on you.) Then they straddle the line in front of you instead of choosing a lane.

The second type is made up of older men and women in little bitty dented cars who drive slower and with an attitude of learned helplessness, like those dogs that get shocked repeatedly in psychology experiments. Their stooped postures and fearful eyes seem to say, "Please don't hit me again."

Last are the scooters and motorcycles. While not as fast as the Fiats, they are much more obnoxious, noisily weaving in and out of traffic, driving the wrong way up one-way roads and driving on sidewalks. We actually saw a guy on a scooter with a propane tank on his lap, weaving in and out of traffic, talking on his cell phone, and smoking all at the same time.

Despite these distractions, Tim seamlessly guided us into the heart of Rome to our hotel near the Vatican. I am proud of my Italian heritage, and I love Roman history, so on the way into the Eternal City, I bored the kids with some fun facts about Rome. "As we make our way from Britain to France to Italy to Slovenia and then to Turkey, we will use four different currencies and five different languages," I said. "In the year 116 A.D. at the height of the Roman Empire, you could have done so with one language—Latin—and one currency. Roads built during that time are still in use today. We still use the Roman calendar and the Roman alphabet."

I explained that the system of Roman government was a model for America's Founding Fathers, complete with a legislative and executive branch. Roman citizens were guaranteed the right to vote and given a fair trial under law. Furthermore, the cast of characters at the end of the Roman Republic is unequaled in history: Julius Caesar, Pompeii, Marcus Cato, and Cicero, to name but a few.

Our first day in Rome, we were scheduled for an audience with the Pope. Jill and I told the kids to be respectful and kiss his ring if he offered it and not to make fun of his hat. We put on our best clothes and arrived early. We didn't expect much from the Pope, just a few minutes of his time. The conversation would have taken two minutes, tops, but there was none of that. It was October 31, the Feast of All Souls, and the Pope's "audience" consisted of our family plus ten thousand other sodden worshippers in rainy St. Peter's Square.

The square itself is beautiful. Huge colonnades fan out from both sides of St. Peter's Basilica in two arcs, symbolic of the arms of the Roman Catholic Church reaching forth to embrace its communicants. The famous square was designed this way so that when people came to see the Pope give a blessing, they feel as though they are inside (even though they aren't). It is a very welcoming effect for one of the least welcoming places on earth. There are no information booths, no maps, no fliers. There are no signs that say, "Welcome, Catholics, to the home of your faith. We are so glad you are here," or even, "Welcome, Catholics, and thanks to you and your ancestors for paying for all this stuff." There are few directional signs and no staff except for security guards, whose arrogance greatly exceeds their expertise.

The foundation of St. Peter's Basilica was laid by Pope Julius II in 1506. Rather than remodel the existing structure, which the Emperor Constantine built on the Circus of Nero a thousand years before, Julius and his architect Bramante designed a new building that would become the biggest church in the world. The centerpiece of the original plan called for a huge tomb not to God or Jesus or even St. Peter but to Pope Julius II himself!

St. Peter's Basilica took 109 years to finish, and the Baroque interior makes the place feel more like a palace than a church. While the final product does not include the memorial to Julius II, the interior is filled with second-rate statues of popes (twenty-five by my count) and also the preserved body of Pope John XXIII. The result is a veritable pope "hall of fame" but much more overstated than the one in Cooperstown.

It fell to Julius's successor Leo X to raise the needed funds to pay for the building of St. Peter's, and he did so largely by the sale of indulgences. Indulgences are the church's equivalent of a "get out of jail free card" from Monopoly.

If you purchased an indulgence, it could be used to: shorten a relative's time in purgatory, buy forgiveness for your very worst sins, or (my personal favorite) buy forgiveness for the sins you want to commit but haven't gotten around to yet. The sale of indulgences infuriated a German monk named Martin Luther and helped lead to the Protestant Reformation (from Eamon Duffy's *Saints and Sinners: A History of the Popes*).

We shook St. Peter's dust from our feet and took a crowded public bus to the Roman Forum. Rome has two subway lines, but neither go anywhere near the Forum. The six-mile bus ride took forty minutes. The bus stop was a few blocks from the Forum, and when we asked for directions (in Italian), we received only disdainful looks.

At the Forum, the kids were ready for dollar snacks. We stopped at a food van, and they ordered a small Gatorade and two soft-serve ice creams. There were no prices posted—that should have been a clue. The total came to seventeen dollars. My change was two Euros short. This happened repeatedly in Rome, and so for the first time on the trip, I began adding up bills and carefully counting my change.

When we left our hotel on a rainy Wednesday afternoon and pulled into heavy Roman traffic, I found myself telling the kids stories not about the city's greatness but about Rome's fall: the preoccupation with grisly spectator sports, failed attempts at nation-building in the Middle East, abolition of mandatory military service. I talked most of all about the arrogance and corruption of its citizens, much of which we had just witnessed firsthand.

De gustibus non est disputandem ("there can be no arguing about matters of taste") is how a Roman would have answered my criticism of the Eternal City. When compared with New York, London, and Paris, Rome didn't measure up, and that was more than just a question of taste. In New York, London, or Paris, we never needed to hire a cab because public transit was sufficient. We rarely needed to ask for directions in those cities, and when we did, people couldn't have been more helpful. If we wanted to buy a Coke or a loaf of bread, we could always find an open shop. And while these other cities have incredible histories, they remain vibrant and very much alive in the present. By all of these criteria— progressiveness, public transport, convenience—Rome fails as a city. All Rome has to offer is faded greatness from the past.

This topic sparked a spirited family discussion. Only the newest member of the family was eerily silent. Tim's video screen showed that our current position was in the middle of London, near Piccadilly Circus to be precise. He must have been dreaming about home. "This map says we're in London. Jesus Christ, of all the times for him to stop working! Now when we need him the most," I said.

After ten minutes of aimless wandering surrounded by revving motorcycles and drivers trying to make four lanes into six, Tim finally got his voice back. "In two hundred meters, bear left," Tim piped up, as though nothing was wrong.

"I have a better idea Tim," I said. "How about in two hundred meters you kiss my ass?"

"David!" Jill interrupted "Watch your mouth."

"In fifty meters turn left," said Tim.

In the backseat Joe started laughing.

"It's not funny, Joe!" I now addressed Jill. "Your boyfriend wants us to turn left in 50 meters, but as you can see there is no bridge so if we listen to him, I'll drown the whole family in the Tiber River."

"I think what he means is that if you go up a little further," said Jill, "we can get turned around and headed back the right way."

"How can you trust this piece of shit after the way he left us hanging?" I asked. "He gained our confidence only to let us down when we need him the most. Tim is in there right now laughing at us. We are getting out of Rome ourselves."

Jill replied, "Well, he wasn't working then and now he is."

"You always take his side!" I sneered. "If he takes us over that river again, I'm throwing him in."

Jill gave up, shook her head, and sighed. We finally made it out of Rome with Tim's help, but things will never be the same between us. In any case, Tim was about to get a long vacation, as we would not need his counsel again until we reached Australia. We sold the van in Rome and hopped on a train for Venice en route to Slovenia.

We arrived in Postojna, Slovenia, at 11 p.m. on a cold November night with no map, no guidebook, and no knowledge of the Slovenian language. (The guidebook had been mailed along with several other items to my relatives in Italy two months ahead of time but never arrived, and we were unable to find a replacement.) Postojna is a small town, and no taxis waited at the train station. After a glance at a map on the door, we gathered our belongings and began rolling our suitcases over the crumbling sidewalks in the direction of town.

We happened upon a hotel that appeared to have been built during the Communist era. Our room smelled like a septic tank, but it was cheap and the desk clerk spoke English. She directed us to a restaurant for a late dinner, where for seven dollars we were served different courses of meats and vegetables. The food was delicious, and when the bill arrived it was tallied correctly—and they gave us proper change. Back at the hotel, we turned on cable TV. "Animal Planet" was on, in English with Slovenian subtitles. The show we watched was about an animal rescue in a dangerous American city—Phoenix, Arizona.

Slovenia was a lovely country and a great travel bargain. Ljubljana, the capital, is a romantic city. A huge castle on a hill above the city is illuminated by violet-colored lights. Sadly, what I most remember about that city is talking on the phone. As we traveled, I always tried to plan two countries ahead, which meant that while in Slovenia I was working on our plans for India. I was trying to book train reservations online from Delhi to Bangalore and getting nowhere. So I tried it over the phone using a VOIP connection and didn't do any better. Frustrated with India's rail system, we decided to fly. After what seemed like an hour, I had made the reservation, but when they ran the credit card they said it wouldn't work. There was no way to hold the reservation so I called the U.S. credit card company, and they put me through to a call center—in Bangalore, India. The representative informed me that the company had "suspicious charges" on my account from Slovenia and attempts to make purchases in India. "I am in Slovenia, and soon we are traveling to India," I said as patiently as possible. "I told your company all this before I left." The man referred me to his supervisor, who told me that my card would be ready to use the next day, which meant I would need to start planning India all over again, this time from Turkey.

CHAPTER 7

TURKEY

Hitting Our Stride among Friends | *November 15–December 9, 2007*

We checked into our hotel in Istanbul and went out for dinner. Tommy was the first family member to enter the restaurant. When the host asked him a question in Turkish, Tommy assumed the man was asking for our name to put on a waiting list.

"Boesch," said Tommy.

The host smiled broadly. He clapped his hands together twice, and three bus boys appeared. The host yelled, "*Besh*" and the busboys went to work preparing a table for five. When the host addressed me in Turkish, he seemed disappointed that I didn't understand him.

On the walk home, we stayed close together. After all, TV shows and magazine articles repeatedly report that "the Islamic world" hates America. We knew Turkey was a moderate country, but we also knew that at the time of our visit the United States' approval rating in Turkey was 10 percent. The war in Iraq had led to a Kurdish uprising on Turkey's southern border. Many Turks felt that this was America's fault. We also knew that Muslims use nasty words like *kaffir* or "infidel" to describe Westerners. We expected the worst.

Outside a small convenience store, Cami stopped to pet an old, arthritic white dog named Dost who lived in a cardboard box. Catching sight of her, the store owner came out with pieces of candy for Joe, Tom, and Cami. The kids had already had their dollar snack (1.5 new Turkish Lira) for the day, so they looked at me to see if it was okay to accept the candy. I nodded. The shop owner went back inside without trying to sell us anything.

Though we did not request a wake-up call, we got one at 4:30 a.m. Our hotel was near the Blue Mosque, and before dawn the muezzin was calling the faithful to get up and pray. Unlike Zanzibar, where the muezzin's call to prayer was a recording, in Istanbul the call was live. Only the best singers were chosen.

To our infidel ears, it sounded like high-pitched moaning, and none of us were very happy about it—especially Cami. She asked, "Dad, can you please tell that muzzer-guy to be quiet? He woke me up this morning, and he is not a good singer."

I answered, "Cami, the man is doing his job. He is reminding people to get up and pray."

She replied, "Why don't they just set an alarm clock?"

Tommy intervened, and it did not help matters: "Cami, I think you only say you hate him but you secretly like him and that he is your boyfriend." Cami, with her blanket still in hand from the night before, put her head down on the breakfast table and cried.

The muezzin calls all of Istanbul's 15 million citizens to prayer five times daily. Many choose not to listen. As with all religions, some practitioners are devout, others lax. The modern Turkish government could not care less, but it wasn't always this way. Turkey was the center of the Ottoman Empire and was ruled under religious law from 1299 until 1923. In 1935, Turkey became a secular country with separation of church and state. Some Islamic sects, such as Sufism, were outlawed altogether.

Sufis are Muslim mystics who pursue a direct, personal understanding of God through a number of mental and physical exercises. One of these methods is a whirling dance intended to plunge the dancer into a state of concentration upon Allah. While the dancer spins round and round, he may see visions of angels. These dancers are the Mawlawiyya whirling dervishes. The Mawlawiyya part of the name derives from the Persian mystical poet Rumi of Mawlana, a dervish himself. *Dar* in Persian means "door," so *darvesh* literally means "the one who goes from door to door." Darveshes went door to door to beg for food because they were so focused on God that they became indifferent to money and material possessions.

Sufism remains outlawed, but if you want to see the "whirling dervishes" you still can. A show is performed nightly in a room at the Istanbul bus station. Clad in long white woolen skirts, the dancers spin round and round continuously for forty-five minutes. I don't know how they kept from getting dizzy. (Perhaps dizziness was the starting point on the road to ecstasy?) The show costs ten dollars per person. Watching the dervishes whirl was interesting and entertaining, but also awkward. We were paying money to watch people practice their religion. Imagine if tourists came to a Catholic church and paid money to watch little old ladies say the rosary. The other possibility is that we were paying to watch them *perform* their religion. All that whirling may not have been meant to put them into an ecstatic union with God, but into a very real union with our money. Or, it could have been a combination of both.

A good litmus test for whether something is culture or just a floor show is to ask this: "Would the people involved be doing the same thing if no one was paying to watch them?" In Tanzania at the "Maasai cultural tour" the answer was simple. They waited for us to arrive then began their phony little dance. With the dervishes it was harder to tell. To find out would have required an interview with questions like: Did you come closer to God? Would you be here tonight if there were no customers?" But none of the dervishes stuck around for questions.

Usually the first one awake in our family, I would spend the early mornings in Istanbul on our hotel's rooftop terrace enjoying the same spectacular view of the Bosporus that Constantine would have seen some two thousand years before. I could have sat there sipping Turkish coffee forever, but Istanbul offers so much to see.

Here is Joe's take on the Hagia Sophia Basilica, believed by many to be the most beautiful building on earth:

In the 6th Century the emperor Justinian built the Hagia Sofia basilica. When Christian rule was overthrown, they changed the basilica to a mosque. There were over 3 million painted gold tiles for the mosaics in the basilica. When the Muslims made it a mosque, they covered up the mosaics. In 1935 when it was made a museum, they took the plaster off the mosaics.

A security guard in the Hagia Sophia caught site of Cami and in a thick Turkish accent asked her name. "Cami." Jill replied.

"No, her name," the guard asked once again, pointing at Cami.

"Cami is her name," Jill replied, puzzled.

The guard offered Cami a piece of hard candy. She then took us upstairs in the Hagia Sophia where Vikings had carved graffiti into the walls. Like all of Istanbul's rulers, the Vikings appreciated its beauty and strategic importance. They called Istanbul "*Milkegard,*" meaning "City of Gold."

Istanbul is situated where the continents of Europe and Asia reach out and almost touch each other, like the fingers of God and Adam in Michelangelo's famous fresco. Like most great cities, Istanbul is meant to be explored on foot. No matter where we walked in Istanbul, we ran into carpet salesmen who gave us variations of the same speech: "Hello friend. What a lovely family you have. I have children too. Please do me the honor of coming into my shop for a cup of tea and we will talk about being a father." They were so charming that it was difficult to decline, but we kept walking . . . and walking.

Tommy described a typical day:

> We walked a very long way through a park and over a bridge. While we were walking through the park and there was this statue of Ataturk. Ataturk is the founder of modern Turkey. Also in the park there was a pretty little fountain. Once we left the park we walked across the bridge. There were so many fishermen crowding around each other trying to get to a better spot and hardly anybody was catching any fish and the fish that they did catch were guppies. Once we got across the bridge over the Golden Horn we walked to a tram that went up a hill to Taksim Square.

At the top of Taksim Square we saw thousands of people wearing black shirts and carrying signs—a demonstration was about to take place. Along the side of the road were riot police carrying shields and wearing helmets. We took refuge on the second-floor patio of a Burger King. From here it was apparent that there were even more riot police, some carrying rifles, on the roofs of various buildings.

Jill and I walked down into the crowd to check things out. Jill asked one of the sign-carrying demonstrators what she was protesting.

"Peace," the woman replied.

"Are you for it or against it?" I asked.

"For it," she replied, before walking down the street with her comrades.

It was rare for our hotel to have children as guests, and ours were treated royally. Uhmet, who worked as the receptionist, taught the kids some Turkish phrases, including how to count to ten. The Turkish word for five is "besh," pronounced exactly like our last name, which explained the excitement of the host at the restaurant on our first night. When he saw five of us and heard Tommy say "Boesch," he assumed we were Westerners who knew Turkish. "Cami" is the Turkish word for mosque. The security guard at the Hagia Sophia could not understand why we kept saying "mosque" when she asked for our daughter's name.

Deniz, the owner of the hotel, took particular interest in the kids, talking politics and history with Joe, playing guitar with Tommy, and showering Cami with gifts, including a new blanket. One night Deniz took Jill and me to a cafe near the hotel. The all-male crowd sat silently smoking flavored tobacco in big hookahs, all eyes turned toward the TV. Turkey was playing Norway in European cup futbol. This should have been a home game for Turkey, but it was moved to Norway because of bad Turkish fan behavior. Norway was leading "one nil," and then Turkey scored. The place erupted into a deafening roar. Turkey went on to win 2–1. We felt so lucky to have been part of a genuine Turkish cultural experience that when we returned to the hotel I set about writing an e-mail to our friends.

I asked Deniz, "How would you describe the teahouse?"

"Kitsch," he replied. "Dressed up to look like the real thing, but definitely not the real thing." Deniz must have seen the disappointment spread over my face. "I'm sorry," he said.

One night Deniz arranged for us to attend a Turkish professional basketball game. The cheerleaders were circa 1980s, with white boots and big hair. The teams, Besiktas and Efes Pilsen, were mediocre. The real show was in the stands. The game was not a sellout, but in the three sections next to ours Besiktas fans (known as Carsi) were crammed into every seat from the floor all the way up to the last row. Dressed in Besiktas colors of black and white, the Carsi screamed and stomped their feet even during mundane parts of the game such as timeouts. They were passionate about something, but that something was not basketball. The Carsi were surrounded on three open sides by riot police just like the ones we had seen the previous day. At halftime, the fans were herded together like prisoners. They were allowed to purchase food at the concession stand but not to mingle with the rest of the crowd.

After the game, thankfully won by Besiktas, we walked under a bridge on our way to the rail station. What we saw caused us to stop dead in our tracks. Next to vendors selling cheese and fish were vendors selling guns: big, shiny .45-caliber handguns.

"Can we get three?" Joe asked.

"No," I replied.

"But the bad guys have them."

"Joe, I have heard that argument before, and we are not getting a gun, let alone three."

I was terrified. How could the police cordon off the Besiktas fans during the game and then allow them to walk out of the arena and buy giant pistols without a five-day waiting period? Would a loss at the basketball game mean blood in the streets?

Back at the hotel, Deniz addressed our concerns. He explained that the Turks weren't crazy enough to let people walk around with real handguns. These were toy guns that were not configured to fire real bullets. People who bought them did so just to look tough. He explained that the Carsi don't care about basketball. Besiktas is the oldest sports club in Turkey and also the country's most popular futbol team. Since the futbol team wasn't playing that night, the Carsi were cheering for their club at the basketball game. Riot police are a good idea, he said, as the Carsi tend to get crazy.

Deniz had read our website and took some offense at our expectations of his country as articulated by Joe's first journal entry:

The place I'm most afraid of is Turkey. It is made up of Muslims and most of them don't like the U.S.

Deniz asked, "Do you feel disliked or threatened here in Turkey?"

I thought about this for a while. The inescapable conclusion was that the Turks' antipathy towards our government did not translate into hostility towards us. This came as a surprise, but it shouldn't have. When I meet someone from South Africa I don't hold her responsible for apartheid. When I meet a German, I don't blame him for the Holocaust. This doesn't make me a broad-minded person, only a rational one. I expected Turks to lack that rationality because they were Muslim.

Mark Twain wrote that "travel is fatal to prejudice," and here, on the rooftop terrace of the Dersaadet Hotel, I found myself forced to reconcile my pre-judged world view with what I saw with my own eyes. "No, Deniz," I replied. "We don't feel threatened. In fact, apart from our own country we feel more welcome here than anywhere else—especially now that you clarified the gun thing."

Feeling comfortable was critical to our next decision. Joe and I wanted to see the Gallipoli Peninsula, but Cami had seen enough battlefields. Thanksgiving was only two days away but contrary to popular belief turkey is not served in Turkey, and without Jill's family the holiday would lose its meaning. So, for the first time since leaving the United States, we decided to split up.

The following morning, the boys and I walked to a travel agency that specialized in tours to just one place: Canakkale, a small town that is the jumping-off point for both Troy and Gallipoli. As we neared the agency, the carpet salesmen changed from their usual sales pitch to this: "G'day mate. Good on ya mate." Gallipoli is a pilgrimage place for Australians, and the salesmen figured that since we were white and heading in the direction of the travel agency, we must be Australian, and so they spoke to us in an idiom we would understand.

We had assumed—incorrectly—that tours would cost one standard price and that with a few clicks of a mouse we would be done. Not so. We had to play the usual Turkish game, which by now I had come to enjoy. First our travel agent had to call the bus company, then he had to call the hostel in Canakkale to see if they had room, and then he gave me a price. I told him that I was not a rich man and stood up to leave. He pleaded for us to stay and got a glass of tea for me and some cocoa for the boys. He called his people back to get the okay for a better price. He then presented this new and improved offer.

I replied that this would be acceptable as long as Tommy could go for half price. More phone calls, more gesturing—but yes, that would be acceptable. We would leave at 6 a.m. the next morning, Thanksgiving Day.

A family with three boys, the youngest of whom was singing a fine rendition of "Sweet Home Alabama," was in the back of the bus on the ride to Canakkale. When Joey and Tommy took out their PSPs and started playing video games, the other boys couldn't resist coming over to have a look. They were from Hobart, Tasmania, and their names were Bryn, Tom, and Simon. The boys were also on a trip around the world with their parents, Helen Parry and Tom Watt.

While Cami and Jill were having Chicken McNuggets back in Istanbul, the Watt family joined the boys and me as we walked the streets of Canakkale, searching for a restaurant. Joe and Tom journeyed ahead, but the Watt family stayed tightly clustered together like we had on our first night in Istanbul. Noticing my glance, Tom said, "We left with three children and we are committed to returning to Australia with three children."

I asked, "Don't they chafe at that?" Bryn was fifteen.

"Occasionally they do," he responded. He then shared their family's experience in Istanbul, which was much less positive than our own. They had made the mistake of going into a carpet shop, where they were hustled into a back room. They had to push their way out. Tom had also been cornered and forced to pay twenty dollars to some street thugs.

The boys and I were in bed that night by 9:00 p.m. At 11:30, I was awakened by car horns blaring and people shouting. I thought it must be a political uprising, and here we were in the middle of it. I watched out the window, expecting Molotov cocktails to be thrown. I knew the rioters would be keen to take American hostages.

It seemed as though our disaster planning that had begun way back in Canada was about to pay dividends. Jill and Cami were still in Istanbul, and the folks at the hotel would protect them and take them to the embassy. The boys and I would barricade ourselves in our room. First I went downstairs to learn more details. I did not wake the boys. When I asked the front desk clerk about all the commotion, he simply pointed to the television. Final score, second round

European cup soccer: Turkey 2, Bosnia 0.

The following morning we took a bus to the ancient city of Troy. Except for the big, modern Trojan horse out front, the place looked like rubble in the middle of a cornfield. Fortunately, our attractive tour guide explained that this was not just a pile of rocks, but nine excavated cities of Troy. The guide said, "In the process of excavating, they destroyed some fine Roman ruins. It's okay though, because in Turkey, Roman times are like yesterday."

I could barely contain myself when I explained to the boys that we were on the very spot where Hector and Achilles worked out their differences. Joe and Tommy know the story of the Trojan War yet they did not share my excitement. In order to humor me, they put away their PSPs and pretended to listen.

After leaving Troy, we crossed the Dardanelles (a.k.a. the Hellespont) by boat en route to the Gallipoli Peninsula. I explained to the kids that in 483 B.C.E., on his way to the battle of Thermopylae, the Persian King Xerxes attempted to cross here by building a bridge of papyrus. When high seas tore apart his bridge, Xerxes beheaded his engineers and then ordered the seas to be lashed three hundred times. His second set of engineers, working under extreme pressure, built a bridge out of ships and Xerxes made it across.

Some 2,398 years after Xerxes, Australian and New Zealand Army Corps (ANZAC) soldiers tried to land at nearly the same place. Like the beaches of Normandy, the beaches at ANZAC Cove are completely exposed. As soon as they left the beach, the ANZACs climbed straight up a steep hill covered with mud and loose rock. I had Joe and Tommy pretend they were Australian marine infantry and try to climb up the hill. This proved very difficult for them, even on a dry sunny day without gunfire. Once the ANZACs reached the top of the hill, they encountered resistance from a small but brave bunch of Turkish troops under the command of Mustafa Kemal-Ataturk—the father of modern Turkey. The ANZACs dug in across from them, marking the beginning of a bloody war of attrition.

The most famous battle occurred at Lone Pine Hill. Here, ANZAC troops were repeatedly sent out of their trenches by an overzealous British officer, only to be mowed down by Turkish machine gun fire. Six months later, the ANZACs abandoned Gallipoli under cover of darkness. The entire enterprise was such a failure that the man responsible lost his job. His name was Winston Churchill.

As we traveled around the world, we toured a lot of battlefields, but Gallipoli was the only one that showed both sides of the story. There were Turkish memorials and ANZAC cemeteries. We crawled through Turkish trenches and

ANZAC trenches. At the museum there were Turkish diaries and letters translated into English and English diaries and letters translated into Turkish.

The Turks lost 55,000 men in the Gallipoli campaign; the British, 21,000. The Australians lost only 7,500 men, yet the campaign had its greatest effect on the Australian national psyche. For the Turks and British this was just another battle in a long history of warfare, but as Tom and Helen explained to us, it was at Gallipoli that Australia became a nation. The Gallipoli Landing is remembered every year on April 25 as ANZAC Day in Australia.

We had a different guide at Gallipoli than at Troy. He was a native Turkish speaker in his forties who knew the facts of the battle well, but he talked funny. The sentence, "So you see, there was a certain amount of uncertainty regarding the location of the boats," was pronounced, "So you seej, jere was a shertain amount of unshertainty regarding ja locajion of ja boaj." Soon all five of the boys were laughing and doing their own impersonations.

So much for being moved by the horror of war.

At times like these, I began to wonder if the whole trip was just a waste of time. I pulled Joe and Tom off to the side and confronted them with a litany of their shortcomings.

"You don't care where Xerxes crossed the Hellespont, you don't care where Hector fought Achilles, you don't even care about where Australia became a nation!" I continued, "All you want to do is spend your days mocking some poor man with a speech impediment who is out here trying to make a living. Grandpa Ed was right. We should have gone to the Epcot Center."

I shared my frustrations with Tom and Helen. "We feel the same way, David," Tom replied. "It is hard to know if they are learning anything at all—but don't you think a deep appreciation of history is a lot to expect at this age?"

We rode the bus back to Istanbul and at the hotel we turned on CNN, where there was a story about the terrible flooding in southwestern Turkey near Bodrum—our next destination. The flooding concerned us, and we considered staying in Istanbul. Deniz offered to call his cousin in Bodrum. The cousin reported that everything was fine, so we said goodbye to our new friends, the Watts, and to the rest of our friends at the Dersaadet Hotel.

Tommy had this to say about Bodrum: *"This place is famous because Cassius and Brutus went there after they murdered Caesar. Also Herodotus father of history was born in bodrum."*

These days, Bodrum is best known for its beaches, and during summer it is packed with European visitors. As we were there in December, Bodrum was empty. We had rented a five-bedroom villa with a pool and a panoramic view of the Aegean for one thousand dollars per week, a savings of three thousand dollars over the summer price.

The kids couldn't wait to swim and were disappointed to find that the pool was green with algae. We tried swimming in the ocean, but that was too cold. Still feeling the need for exercise, I set up a calisthenics course on the lawn. We rotated through push-ups, sit-ups, dips, and jumping-jack stations. At each station the kids would count their repetitions in Turkish: *Bir, iki, ooch, dord, besh.*

Tommy's hair was getting shaggy. I had read how haircuts vary greatly from one country to another. In Turkey, a haircut is traditionally followed by a hard twist of the neck until it snaps. Tommy remembered my dad's neck injury and was terrified that he was going to leave the barbershop paralyzed. He wouldn't consent to a haircut until we made the barber promise not to snap his neck. While Tommy got his haircut, Jill and I took Cami to look for postcards. When we returned to the barbershop, Tommy was thankfully still moving his arms and legs, but it looked as though a cross-eyed kindergartener had cut Tommy's hair. Some spots were nearly bald, others were sticking straight up and still others were as long as when Tommy sat down. The barber was quite proud of his efforts and happily posed for photos.

Women know not to criticize someone's hairstyle, no matter how horrible. "It looks good, Tom," Jill said.

"I like it," Cami said.

Joe was not so diplomatic. "Tommy, that is the crappiest haircut I have ever seen, and it makes your head look even more gigantic than it actually is."

Tommy cares a lot about his appearance. His bad haircut—and maybe his brother's remarks—made him cry.

Bodrum is built on a beautiful harbor, and overlooking the harbor is a castle originally built by the Knights Templar. The castle houses a museum of underwater archaeology, which includes the ruins of a shipwreck from 3000 B.C.E. Like most museums in Turkey this one was free for the kids. Furthermore, the kids were allowed to climb on the marble Roman sculptures, the kind of sculptures that would be roped off in most countries, but not in Turkey, where Rome is "like yesterday."

We enjoyed our week of rest in Bodrum, where the big villa allowed us to spread out and have some time alone. Soon, the week was over and it was time to fly to our third stop in Turkey—Cappadocia.

Remember earlier in this book when I cited the chance of being killed in a single airplane flight is 1 in 10.46 million if you are traveling on one of the world's 25 safest airlines? I am a man of science and was greatly reassured by these statistics—until the morning we were flying to Cappadocia on an airline we had never heard of. Jill and I were up early, and we saw on TV that an airline flying on a similar route to ours had crashed and all fifty-four passengers were killed. It is hard to be rational when confronted with the nauseating realization that "that could have been us." We didn't tell the kids, but Jill and I glanced nervously at one another with every jolt on that bumpy flight.

As with Bodrum, it was off-season in Cappadocia. The owner of our hotel had even contacted us to ask if we could find somewhere else to stay. We were the only guests scheduled for that week, so if we canceled he could send his staff home and avoid having to pay them. He later wrote back to say he had changed his mind and we would still be welcome.

The Cappadocia region is unique, in large part due to its geology. The rock is a very soft type of sandstone, and caves can easily be carved from it. Many buildings in Cappadocia, including our hotel, are cave dwellings. We were reminded of this whenever we bumped our heads on the ceiling, and a shower of small rocks came down.

We spent our days hiking alone in the snow or rain, moving from one cave dwelling to the next, never knowing what we would find. The kids loved our explorations—especially Tommy, who has always liked crawling into tight spaces.

Here is what he wrote about a typical day:

> We went to some incredible caves in Cappadocia. When we were up there, Joey and I showed them the tunnel. I got a better flashlight and crawled through it. I didn't get to the end because it got too small. Cami was to scared to go in and mom tried to crawl through but she didn't make it much further than me.

Cami had this to say:

> today we want on a hike at Cappadocia. Cappadocia is a place where pepole dig to make houses. thay carve the houses in this rock 60 million years ago. it was cool because of the shapes of the rocks. the hike was hard to get up and down the hill. thare was a little skinny tunnel that mom and Tommy went in. thay thought it was cool. We had lots of fun at Cappadocia.

The International UFO Museum fit right in with the bizarre geologic landscape of Cappadocia. Perhaps the thinking here is that, if like us, aliens covet the familiar when seeking out a landing spot, Cappadocia might look the most similar to home. The museum was closed, but Cami saw a litter of puppies outside and went to pet them.

"Careful Cami," said Joe. "Those are alien puppies from outer space."

Our home from May to September

Lunch with Father Welsch. Crown Candy Kitchen, St. Louis, Missouri

Our first international stop, Victoria, British Columbia

Outside the Baseball Hall of Fame, Cooperstown, New York

Mr. Bossone teaches the kids how to make pizza, Squan Tavern, Manasquan, New Jersey

Getting ready to go, September 12, 2007

A Maasai tribesman gives Cami a lift through "the pokies"

Cami and Tommy join some of the local children in front of the N'gresi clinic

Safari campsite, Serengeti National Park, Tanzania

Atop the Ngorongoro Crater

Joe and Tommy swim with sea turtles in Zanzibar

With Paul Azzara at Mont Saint Michel

Tommy does some math, Massa Lubrense, Italy, October 2007

Whirling dervishes, Istanbul, Turkey

Tommy's "worst haircut ever," Bodrum, Turkey

Crossing the Hellespont, Canakkale, Turkey

Camel riding, Urgup, Turkey (Cappodocia region)

Boesch Family Yoga, Varkala, India

Snake charmer, Cochin, India

Dubare elephant camp, Mysore, India

Christmas with Sister Hildegarde and Sister Santosh, St. Philomena's Church, Mysore India

With Colonel Dr. A.C. Suryanarayanan, Shanta (center, standing), and family, Mysore, India

Bangkok, Thailand

Jill gives an orange to a monkey, Chiang Mai, Thailand

"Monk Chat" with Tom and Jerry, Chiang Mai, Thailand

Snorkeling on Tommy's tenth birthday, Railay Beach, Thailand

Cami's broken leg, Shinto Shrine, Tsuruga, Japan

Cami dressed as a maiko, Kyoto, Japan

Tommy surfs in Caloundra, Queensland, Australia

Byron Bay, New South Wales, Australia

"Overhead Damage," Broken Head, New South Wales, Australia

The Southern Ocean, Bruny Island, Tasmania, Australia

Joe bungy jumps off the Kawarau Bridge, Queenstown, New Zealand

Bakery, Bariloche, Argentina

Monte Cerro Fitzroy, El Chaltén, Argentina

Perito Moreno Glacier, El Calafate, Argentina

The Chilean fiords as seen from the Navimag Ferry

Osorno Volcano, Puerto Varas, Chile

"Shed Penguin," Ancud,
Chiloé Island, Chile

Joe prepares to eat raw sea cucumber, Cucao, Chiloé Island National Park, Chile

Climbing Volcan Villarica, Pucon, Chile

CHAPTER 8

INDIA

A Bout of Culture Shock | *December 7–26, 2007*

*O*ur hotel promised to send a big car. We could identify the driver because he would be holding a sign with our name on it. For years, I have
seen limo drivers waiting outside airport security, holding cardboard
signs for big-shot executives. This was the first time that someone would be holding a sign just for us. The excitement I felt was almost enough to overcome the
exhaustion of the previous night's travel.

Most international flights in Asia take place at night, and our Turkish Airways flight from Istanbul to Delhi was no exception. After we reached cruising altitude the flight attendants disappeared. We did not see or hear from them again
the rest of the flight. They did, however, leave the beverage carts in the middle
of the aisle, allowing free access to the liquor. About 2 a.m., Jill was trying to
get some sleep when a fat drunk Indian stood over her seat and began yelling at
someone several rows in front of him. Jill awoke with a start. I jumped out of my
seat and told the man to shut up. I expected a fight, but much to my surprise, he
sheepishly sat down and stayed quiet.

There was no announcement as we began our descent into Delhi, and as we
landed some of the drunken passengers were still standing in the aisle. Before the
captain had turned off the "fasten seat belt" sign indicating it was safe to move
about the cabin, hordes of people were already crowding toward the exit. We were
fortunate to be seated near the front of the plane and were among the first to go
through the "foreigner" line at Passport Control. The agent was wearing a dirty
suit and had long hairs growing out of his nose. Joe asked if he was going to
stamp our passports or wipe a booger in them.

Our plan was to spend three weeks exploring the southwest part of India. We
would fly directly from Delhi to Bangalore, travel southwest to Cochin, and then
back north to Mysore, where we would spend Christmas with a colleague's parents.

It was 6 a.m., and our plan was in jeopardy because we had a domestic connection to catch from Delhi to Bangalore, scheduled to depart in forty-five minutes from an entirely different airport ten miles away. A shuttle bus connected the two airports, but it didn't begin running for another hour. We needed a taxi.

Outside the Delhi airport, the sun was barely beginning to rise and we could see a black cloud of pollution. It tasted like soot. The cabbies who campaigned for our business tried to tell us this was "mist." We quickly loaded our luggage into an old SUV and after riding two hundred yards, we had a flat tire. The cabbie radioed for someone else to take us—and then had the nerve to ask me for a tip.

We arrived at the domestic terminal at 6:30 a.m. and ran through a huge crowd of people to the front of the line. I stayed with the kids while Jill made eye contact and waved our boarding passes—which I had printed in Istanbul—at a Jet Airways employee on the other side of the security checkpoint. She escorted us to the front of the security line. We ran through the "mist" onto the tarmac and were the last to board our plane. The Jet Airways aircraft was brand new, sparkling clean, and the food was great. Maybe our first impression of India was an anomaly, or it was just a bad day in Delhi.

As we exited the Bangalore airport, we told the kids to keep a tight hold on their bags and to look for our name on a sign. To our surprise, there were dozens of sign-holding drivers standing in the rain, and dozens of unaffiliated drivers vying for our business. Some individuals just wanted the opportunity to carry our bags in hopes of earning a tip. When one of them tried to take Cami's bag, she pulled it back, shaking her head. Jill spotted a man holding a sign board that read "Booshs" in runny black marker.

The "big car" the hotel sent was a sedan the size of a Toyota Corolla. There were no seat belts, and only two of our suitcases fit in the trunk. The rest were either sitting on our laps or strapped to the top of the vehicle. As we exited the airport and came to an intersection, a traffic cop with a whistle held up his hand for us to stop, but our driver, who until that moment had seem like a reasonable man, suddenly transformed into Mario Andretti with a full bladder. He blew right by the policeman, darting right and left on the rain-slicked streets in between tuk tuks and mopeds.

We were not traveling very fast, perhaps only thirty miles an hour, but the driver's reluctance to use brakes or turn signals and his constant horn-blowing caused us to feel that we were careening out of control. After two minutes, about as long as a typical roller coaster ride, we stopped as quickly as we started, stuck behind a huge line of cars. As we Booshs waited in traffic, we saw all the modern office high-rises we expected from a "high tech" city, but the old mingled with the new. Donkey carts shared the road with brand-new Mercedes. We saw a skinny brown man leading a skinny brown cow with a rope, and from time to time he would stoop beneath an udder and give it a squeeze in order to get a drink.

The eight-mile trip from the airport to our hotel took forty minutes. Our hotel was a clean and comfortable refuge, and we lay down for a rest. A scream woke me from my nap. I ran to the other room to find Tommy rolling on the floor and crying hysterically, his hands near an electrical outlet.

Here is Tommy's description:

In Bangalore, you could say there was electricity in the air. I plugged something in and got shocked by 230 volts. I think the only pain that could be worse than that would be a higher number of volts. This is what it felt like; there was a buzz and pure pain shot up my fingers then I couldn't feel any part of my body, then every bone in my body started tingling followed by pure pain.

When I was shocked I cried for 2 reasons; Because I thought "I'm done for I'm not going to get to see the rest of the world, I have to die in this God forsaken place and when I am dead my brother and sister will be furious because I ended the trip." The second reason I was crying was because it hurt so, so, so, so, so, so, so, so, so, so, so bad. I was lucky I survived.

As soon as Joe realized that Tommy wasn't dead, he began laughing uncontrollably. "Is that what you call culture shock, Tommy?" Joe launched into his own pantomime version of the electrocution, flailing his arms and rolling on the floor.

Tommy was in need of comfort. The hotel had a pool, so after he settled down, we put on our swimsuits and went downstairs. The pool was large, shallow, and oddly devoid of swimmers. A security guard in a fancy brown uniform and a hat guarded the entrance. I showed him our room key and walked in.

"I need your passport," said the guard.

"But we are going swimming. Why would I bring a passport?" I asked.

"I need your passport," he replied.

I went back to the room and fetched our passports. When I returned to the pool a second security officer had arrived. Under his watchful eye, the first guard dutifully copied down not just our names but also the passport numbers and place of issuance, so that if anyone needed to know exactly who was in the pool on that December night, they would have the information.

· After our swim, we returned to the room to find the Indian equivalent of *American Idol* on TV. Unlike in the United States, the contestants wore strange costumes and danced as much as they sang. Just like back home, there were two nice judges and one who was saucy and hard to please. The judges spoke mostly Hindi, but sometimes they would switch mid-sentence to English and then back to Hindi. A sentence might begin with unintelligible language, switch to "You were very sexy and you scored well," and then be followed by more unintelligible language.

Jill asked, "Did he just say, 'You were very sexy'?"

"I think so," I replied.

Hindi sounds like jibberish to our ears, but if by some miracle we learned to speak Hindi, it is quite possible the Indian we were talking to wouldn't understand us, as he or she might only know Tamil or Kannada. This is akin to someone from Oregon not being able to understand someone from Alabama. India has twenty-two official languages. English is one of them. We were told time and again that English is all you need to know to get by in India, but this is not entirely true. When asked if they speak English, Indians don't want to disappoint you, so they uniformly say, "Yes."

Body language adds to the confusion. A nod of the head means "yes" and a shake of the head means "no" the world over—but Indians add a variation. They rhythmically abduct and adduct their head from side to side. This is known as the "head bobble." Sometimes this gesture means "yes," sometimes "no," and sometimes "maybe." The meaning is not reflected in wobble frequency or amplitude—or at least as best as we could decipher.

Being misunderstood is far worse than being not understood. Not understood means a blank look or a shrug of the shoulders. Misunderstood means your interlocutor provides you with the false reassurance of an answer to a partially understood question—a potentially dangerous set of circumstances. Jill learned this on her shopping excursion later that evening. The twenty-five dollars we paid for the airport transfer included the use of the car and the driver for the entire day. After dropping us at the hotel, the same driver who had shown such urgency to get us there had spent the rest of the day lounging in his car and reading the newspaper in the hotel driveway. Jill asked him to take her Christmas shopping.

The driver brought her to the entrance of the big mall on Mahatma Gandhi Boulevard. Jill said, "I should be shopping for about two hours. When I am done, do I meet you here?"

"Yes," the driver replied, with a bobble of his head.

After two hours of fruitless shopping, Jill returned to the meeting place, but the driver was nowhere to be found. It was dark, hot, and crowded. Jill didn't know the address of our hotel, and she didn't have a way to call us. She waited. An hour later, the angry driver turned up. He had been waiting at a different mall exit.

In other countries we visited, it was clear that people didn't speak English, and we didn't expect them to. We got by with phrase books or with studying the language ahead of time. In India, we learned to get by through asking "bobble-proof" questions that required an explanation as opposed to a "yes" or "no." For example, instead of asking, "Is the bus stop this way?" we learned to ask, "Where is the bus stop?"

From Bangalore, we flew to Varkala, on the southwest tip of India and one of India's finest beach towns. I joined the boys bodysurfing in the big waves of the Laccadive Sea. The water was warm, brown, and seemed incapable of supporting life. Occasionally I would step on something sticky and gooey, placental in texture. I don't want to know what it was—ever. To our shock, two huge dolphins jumped and flipped in unison less than one hundred yards from shore. People on the beach screamed and erupted in applause.

When I returned from the sea, two locals were standing in front of Jill and Cami, trying to sell them something. India is only one-third the size of the United States, but it is home to more than 1.1 billion people. At times, it seemed as though every single one of them was trying to sell us something.

The world over, people who try to take advantage of you always have the same shtick. It goes like this:

A smiling local approaches you and begins the conversation with questions such as "Where are you from?" (inevitably they will have a brother or cousin from your town), "How long are you in India?" "How long are you traveling?" These questions are designed to gauge how naive you are and how much money you have. If I say, "We have been here four days. I'm from America. I'm a doctor traveling for a year with my family," the translation may be "Here, just take my checkbook and write down whatever you want."

To combat this, I came up with this plan:

Local: "Where are you from?"

Me: "Bolivia."

Local, looking confused: "How long are you here?"

Me: "As long as it takes." (This has a badass ring to it.)

Local: "What type of work do you do?"

Me: "I'm a shepherd. I tend my sheep."

I tried this approach in Turkey, but the people there were charming, and I felt bad about not telling them the truth. In India, this was not an issue. The touts such as the ones on the beach were aggressive and rude. The sense of shame or privacy that prevents most Westerners from staring too long or from walking up to a stranger is utterly absent in India, so I said this all the time without the slightest amount of guilt.

One Thursday, I needed a cab ride to an ATM machine because our hotel only took cash and the owner insisted on being paid every day. The driver asked for 150 rupees. After ten minutes in the hot sun, I bargained him to eighty rupees, which is what everyone pays. The next day, I needed to go to town again, and the negotiation about the fare was repeated. On Saturday, the same driver and I once again had the same conversation. Why was this charade necessary? He was happy with eighty rupees and so was I, so why not just say so?

I am a peaceful man. I haven't been in a fistfight since freshman year of high school, but on that Saturday afternoon I found myself wanting to beat this man and realized that doing so would make me very happy. I clenched my right hand into a fist, lowered and moved to within an inch of his face. Speaking slowly, I said, "I'll pay eighty rupees. Is that clear?" He ran to start the cab.

That night at dinner I was still fuming.

"Look how angry you still are," Jill said. "Why do you insist on spending ten minutes to bargain a cab ride from four dollars to two dollars, a cab ride that would cost you fifteen dollars in New York? Cab drivers in India make very little, and they are working instead of begging. Why not give the working poor the benefit of the doubt?"

"I see your point," I replied, "but we are in a culture where bargaining is a way of life. To not bargain is to be fleeced and to be fleeced is to be made a fool, and I will not be made a fool. Besides, these are not 'working poor.' These people are predatory."

"You really hate Indians, don't you Dad?" Joe asked.

"I hate those who try to take advantage of guests."

"At least the change has been right," Joe replied.

"What do you mean?" I asked.

"All the haggling takes place up front and once a price is agreed to, it's honored. There aren't hidden service charges and stuff like that—like in Italy."

He was right, but I didn't want to hear it. Nor did I want to hear anything positive about India or its citizenry. I have always thought that culture shock meant experiencing a state of confusion because you were "shocked" by the change in culture, as when we walked in amazement down the streets of Dubai after coming from Tanzania.

That is not the case.

As Daniel Hess stated in *The Whole World Guide to Culture Learning*: "Culture shock involves emotional and physical responses to the accumulated stresses and strains that stem from being forced to meet one's everyday needs in unfamiliar ways. Symptoms include fatigue and discomfort, generalized frustration, excessive fear of being cheated, robbed, or injured (which results in negative feelings toward hosts and a refusal to learn their language or practice their common courtesies), irritability at slight provocations, criticism and fits of anger over delays and other minor frustrations." Had there been a hospital in India for people suffering from culture shock, I would have been in intensive care.

We sent an e-mail to our friend Deniz in Istanbul to tell him of our troubles in India. Next, we called home. We learned that our dog Cookie was sick and would need to be euthanized. I telephoned the family we planned to stay with in Mysore, and they didn't understand a word I said except for "Sujatha," which is my friend's name.

At dinner, Jill looked at me over an uneaten dinner of curried vegetables, bobbled her head, and said, "All I want for Christmas is to get out of India."

It was December 12. We had been in India only six days, and we talked about leaving right then. Our airline allowed free changes, but only had availability on December 14 or 26. Jill and I both decided to leave on the fourteenth, but Joe objected. "I just really want to stay with Sujatha's family," he said. "That's the opportunity of a lifetime and I know things will get better."

I called Sujatha's family again, and again I failed to communicate with the person who answered the phone. I e-mailed Sujatha. "Sue," I wrote, "thanks for the offer but we are really struggling here and no one in your family speaks English." She replied that they speak wonderful English and were waiting for me to call. I told her I had been calling, but Sue insisted her parents had not heard from me.

It turned out I was calling the wrong number. When I called the correct number, Sujatha's mom, Shanta, couldn't have been more delightful, and she spoke English beautifully. We agreed to meet them on December 18 and planned to leave India on the 26th. After a three-day cruise aboard a rice barge through the backwaters of Kerala, we made our way to Cochin, a port city made famous by the Portuguese spice trade in the 1700s.

December is India's coolest month, but it was hot in Cochin. One day we took a cab from the dive we were staying in to a nice hotel, where we paid a fee of five dollars apiece to use the pool. As usual, we had to fill out paperwork and show our passports.

Instead of taking a taxi back to the hotel, we decided to take a ferry across Cochin harbor. We bought tickets for two rupees (about five cents). A dead goat lay rotting in the water as we waited for the boat in the hot afternoon sun. We were among the first people to get on board, and soon the ferry was filled to capacity. We expected the ferry to depart soon, but it didn't.

As more and more passengers climbed aboard, we were squeezed closer and closer together. The ferry was sinking lower and lower in the water, and soon the old wooden gunnels flaked with white paint were only one foot higher than the sea. The heat, the noise of the old diesel motor, and the smell of the exhaust blended with the stench of the rotting goat. Also, the awkwardness of squeezing tightly against sweaty strangers proved overwhelming.

Finally, the boat began to move, and the gentle breeze it created made us feel better. The water of Cochin harbor was black with pollution. Leaning over the rail, Jill and I talked about the horrible death we would all face if the ferry sank. Even if we would have been able to swim to safety, the non-swimmers on the boat would have dragged us down to our deaths. Fortunately, the fifteen-minute ferry journey was uneventful.

As we walked back along the bay, we saw a skinny man sitting cross-legged on the cobblestone street. Three wicker baskets were arranged in front of him. He made eye contact with me and then slowly lifted the top off one of the baskets. Out popped a cobra.

"Aaaaah! Snake!" I yelled.

The kids laughed and so did the snake charmer. He didn't speak English but his business manager, who was just behind him, did. Negotiations for the snake show started at five hundred rupees, but after fifteen minutes of haggling, we settled on one hundred.

The cobras swayed and the kids took their turns posing for pictures behind the snake charmer. While playing the flute on a single breath, he coaxed the snakes one by one back into their baskets. After playing for three minutes, two of the snakes were safely under their lids. Then the snake charmer ran out of wind. The music stopped. The cobra struck. I have never seen a creature move so fast and with such efficiency as cobra number three, and it was not finished. After biting the snake charmer on the left leg, the cobra resumed an upright posture, hood unfurled, hovering, deciding whether to strike again. For his part, the snake charmer calmly returned the flute to his mouth. After a few more minutes of playing, he soothed the cobra into its basket.

In the United States, I would have called an ambulance. Cochin doesn't have them.

"We have to get him to a hospital," I said.

"No, it will be OK," his business manager replied, smiling.

"I'm a doctor, and I don't think it will be OK," I said. "The treatment is antivenom administered in a timely fashion." I raised my voice. "This is not funny."

"It's OK, he is bitten ten times a day," replied the business manager.

"How come he is not dead ten times a day?" I asked.

"Because he milks the venoms from the snake ten times a day," he replied.

Venoms or no venoms, it still looked painful. That was a big snake, and it had bitten the man's leg hard. We paid the snake charmer twice the agreed upon amount, and he was greatly pleased.

Cochin's airport is about fifteen miles out of downtown, and we arrived early for our 6 a.m. flight to Bangalore. The airport was modern and meticulously clean, as was the aircraft that was flying us back to Bangalore. It even had first-run movies. "Too bad this plane has to land," Cami said.

We were back in Bangalore, where the hubbub that had greeted us when we first landed was unchanged, but it no longer bothered us. The taxi drivers who were so aggressive only ten days before now left us alone. I guess they noticed something in our body language that told them we had been in India for a while.

We did have other problems. Our credit card had once again been shut down due to "suspicious charges." I was used to this, so I tried the ATM, but it was broken. We tried getting a cash advance on our ATM card but that didn't work either. Then I remembered the one hundred dollars my boss had given me, still tucked away in my wallet.

That allowed me to pay, with money to spare, for the two-hour ride from Bangalore to Mysore, where we were welcomed by Sujatha's parents, Colonel A. C. Suryanarayanan and his wife, Shanta. Joining us were Sujatha's brother, Colonel Murli, and his wife, Deepa, and their two daughters, Aditi (age eight) and Anushka (a very active two).

Colonel Surya is a retired army surgeon who served in the 1971 India-Pakistan War. With a grey beard and a warm smile, he was dressed in a traditional Indian *dhoti*. He possessed a deep understanding of history and literature and a gravitas that comes with having lived a full and thoughtful life. Murli also was an Indian Army colonel, but his specialty was communications. He was on leave from an assignment in Northern India. As a colonel, he was used to commanding men. People listened to him—he has a special army voice that "makes men quake"—but when used on two-year-old Anushka, his deep-throated "Anu, come here now" got my attention but only made Anushka laugh.

Colonel Surya's wife, Shanta, is a beautiful, youthful woman who begins each day with Hindu prayers and yoga. She sensed right away that we were struggling with India and did her best to make us feel at home. Shanta's real goal during our week visiting her was to find something Cami would eat. Shanta is vegetarian and Cami does not like vegetables in her life, unless you count French fries. Shanta tried everything she knew, including chutney, mild curry, even homemade chapatti, which is an unleavened bread. I thought all the food was delicious, but Cami would not budge. She ate plain rice and bull's eyes (which are eggs cooked in the middle of a piece of bread) for an entire week.

On December 23, we went to Sunday Mass at St. Philomena's, one of the oldest churches in all of India. The original church was built more than two hundred years ago, and the Gothic-style church that stands on the site now was built in the 1930s. The bishop of Mysore said Mass, switching back and forth from English to Kannada (just like the judges on *Indian Idol*), one of the local languages of southern India.

Even with half the service said in a foreign tongue, being in a Catholic church was comforting. Mass is structured the same the world over, and stained glass, communion, incense, and priestly robes also are the same. The bishop finished his sermon with my favorite prayer, St. Ignatius Loyola's Prayer of Generosity:

Lord, teach us to be generous
To give and not to count the cost
To fight and not to heed the wounds
To toil and not to seek for rest. . . .

After Mass, Jill asked if the church had an affiliated orphanage. We were directed across a dirt courtyard to a small brown building. We knocked on a door and waited. No one answered. As we walked away, we heard the door handle turn and a hinge creak. In the doorway stood Sister Hildegarde and Sister Santosh, two middle-aged Ursuline Franciscan nuns dressed in simple, light brown habits. We introduced ourselves and they invited us inside.

The nuns took us past a big dimly lit room with cots packed close together. Most of the cots were empty, but two were occupied by boys sick with fever. I explained that I was a doctor and offered to examine them, but she said they were "doing better, and besides I think one of them is faking." A small box was at the foot of each cot.

We walked on to a small office with room for only four people. Jill and I went inside while the kids waited with a group of six orphans who had gathered to see what the nuns were doing. Sister Santosh served us tea while Sister Hildegarde told us all about St. Philomena's orphanage. They had a total of forty boys in the orphanage. A girls' orphanage was located nearby. Children in orphanages in India are educated differently from children who pay to go to the school. Most of the orphans finish school at about age thirteen and then go out on their own. The boxes at the foot of the cots contain all their possessions. Sisters Hildegarde and Santosh cooked and cleaned for all forty boys, broke up fights, and made sure they did their schoolwork.

Jill told the nuns that our family wanted to "play Santa Claus" for the kids and deliver presents to them on Christmas morning. Sister Hildegarde liked Jill's idea but cautioned that even though in most cases the children's parents were either dead or imprisoned, most of the orphans would likely spend the day with relatives. She suggested we come by the next day to see how many children were at the orphanage. Our own children were excited about the project, and the thought of helping the less fortunate really raised our spirits.

When we returned to St. Philomena's the next morning, the nuns told us that all the children had been picked up. With no orphans to buy gifts for, the kids needed something to cheer them up, and a trip to Mysore's new water park seemed like the next best thing. We flagged down a tuk tuk, and the five of us piled in.

The theme of the Mysore water park is "Red Indian," or what we would call Native American. Near the entrance, Indian kids were dancing atop a huge statue of Sitting Bull while a waterfall cascaded down off of his lap. At the wave pool, hundreds of women clad in saris and men with long pants and sleeveless shirts danced to tinny Indian music in the shallow end.

Joe and Tommy jumped right in. School-age Indian kids are not shy, and Tommy was soon surrounded by Indian boys. A "hello" was followed by a splash in the face, as were questions such as "What is your name?" and "Where are you from?" Tommy couldn't answer a single question because they kept splashing him. We could see his anger growing, and then Joe yelled for Tommy to come to the deep end, a refuge from the madness because none of the Indian kids knew how to swim.

Cami was feeling nauseous, so she stayed with Jill while the boys moved on to a short water slide. Two teenage Indian boys in long pants slid down. Once they had safely reached the bottom, they popped up and began dancing. A park employee dressed in shorts and a long-sleeved shirt waded at the bottom of the slide, continually blowing her whistle, frantically motioning for them to move out of the way. Just like the traffic cop in Bangalore, she was ignored.

Joe stood atop the water slide next to a sign that read "Foot first slidings only." After patiently waiting thirty seconds, Joey bobbled his head from side to side, looked at me, flashed a big grin, and then barreled head first down the slide. The dancing teens saw him coming but it was too late. Just before impact Joe turned his body sideways and cut the legs out from under both boys. The teens went down in a heap, and I thought we were in for a fight, but they came out of the water laughing and finally moved out of the way. Tommy joined in the action, and this scene—which never failed to entertain—was repeated over and over until we left the water park at 4 p.m.

Outside the gates, we began negotiating a ride home with a group of tuk tuk drivers. Apparently they had formed a cartel because the same ride that had cost us 50 rupees on the way there was now to cost us 250 on the way home. If we wanted the comfort of a taxi, that could be ours for a mere 500 rupees.

Jill was furious. "Fine," she fumed. "We will walk."

We began the three-mile trek toward home. The tuk tuk drivers started to laugh at us, and that made Jill even more angry. I considered reminding her to "help the working poor," but I thought better of it. Two blocks up the road, a rogue tuk tuk driver who was not part of the cartel came by and agreed to take us home for 150 rupees. We showed him the address and he said he knew where it was, but twenty minutes later, we were still weaving around Mysore.

Shanta had loaned us her cell phone, so I called our hosts. Colonel Surya answered. I then handed the phone to the driver. The driver relayed our cross streets to the colonel and then handed the phone back to me. The colonel said, "The driver is drunk. Don't tip him. Tell him to drive you three blocks straight ahead. Then get out of the tuk tuk, and walk left two blocks and you will be at our house. Don't tip him. You need to hurry—Ashwiri is going to be here in twenty minutes."

Ashwiri is a reporter from the *Star of Mysore* newspaper. Shanta had called to tell her that an American family was traveling around the world, and she wanted to interview us. Ashwiri was prompt and prepared. She had spent hours looking at our website and had read all the kids' journals. Many people had gone around the world, but the presence of our kids made our story unique. She realized that and spent most of the interview trying to understand the kids' perspectives. Joey and Tommy did great, but Cami was now running a fever.

Colonel Surya and Shanta had found a small Christmas tree that they put up in our room, and that night the kids made snowflake ornaments that we tied onto the tree with string. The English-speaking Mass was the next morning at 7 a.m., so we went to bed early, but before we did, we hung our sweat socks by the kitchen in hopes of Santa's arrival.

All of us climbed into the two beds in the bedroom. At 3 a.m. and again at 5, Cami awoke to vomit. She was complaining of abdominal pain, and looking pale in her yellow Sponge Bob nightie. I examined her. Cami was exceedingly tender at a place midway between her belly button and her right hip, "McBurney's point" in medical parlance. In conjunction with her other symptoms, that meant only one thing: acute appendicitis. Jill took a big breath and through tears explained to Cami that she was going to need an operation. Cami looked at her and said, "It's okay, mom. I hurt in that spot because that is where Anushka bit me." I lifted up Cami's gown to find a human bite mark directly overlying her appendix.

We breathed a sigh of relief and gave Cami some medicine for nausea and then went to Mass. We arrived early to find the crowd was already overflowing out of St. Philomena's. These were not Christians, but Hindus. They did not receive communion but afterwards lined up to touch the ceramic baby Jesus in the manger of the courtyard outside the church.

After Mass we joined Sister Hildegarde and Sister Santosh. Christmas for them meant a rare day off, with no children and time to spend at their brand new convent. It had been dedicated by the bishop on November 18, but this would be their first night staying there. The first meal they cooked at the convent was a breakfast of peppers and eggs for us.

Later, we opened our presents. We got Tommy a statue of Ganesh (the elephant god with many arms) and Cami a mirror with a drawing of the goddess Lakshmi (she brings wealth). Santa brought a knife from Kashmir for Tommy, a watch with changeable bands for Cami, and a stackable Uno game for Joey. None of the kids were very excited about their gifts, and it just didn't feel like Christmas.

Cami took a long nap, and when she awoke she felt much better. Christmas afternoon we drove to the Nesso perfume factory owned by Shanta's cousin, Mr. T. Gowrishankar. He told us all about the manufacturing process and the perfection of a fragrance, from flower to perfume: Within hours of being picked, tons of flowers are transported to the factory, where they are distilled in huge metal vats into a resin that, in turn, is distilled even further into a liquid. The final distillate is analyzed with a modern gas chromatograph and then sold to French perfume buyers. "All perfume goes through France," he said. We learned that a good fragrance evolves with time. It has a beginning, a middle, and an end and should smell a little different along the way. Thanks to the gas chromatograph, counterfeiters could cheaply recreate the initial smell of the perfume but not the evolving scents.

On the ride home we talked about how much courage and discipline must have been involved in running that factory. Dirt roads, an unreliable power supply, dependence on weather, and dealing with condescending Western purchasers all is part of the business, and all this is to make a product that will be consumed by wealthy, vain foreigners.

The following day was our time to leave India. After saying goodbye to Colonel Surya and Shanta, we stopped one last time at the orphanage. Sister Hildegarde answered the door with the *Star of Mysore* in hand, and she pointed to the center page, which featured Ashwiri's article along with pictures of our family.

On the way back to Bangalore, Jill had this to say:

As I gazed out the window, all of a sudden I felt nostalgic. At first I had to ask myself what was I feeling? It sure as hell couldn't be nostalgia! I have been anxious to get out of this place since I arrived . . . counting the days. But, suddenly, I couldn't appreciate enough everything I was seeing. I was disappointed in myself for wasting the past three weeks counting the days until we were due to depart for Thailand. I felt I had let the kids down and threw away a wonderful opportunity. I wondered where in the world we ever would see anything like this place again? I kept thinking of the strip malls on every corner in Mesa.

If a tiger escapes from the zoo on Sunday night, the first place to look for him on Monday morning is back in his cage. We think of zoos as cruel places that cage magnificent wild beasts that yearn to run free. Evidence suggests otherwise. Animals covet predictability—their own territory, a reliable source of food and water, familiar neighbors, etc. So, an animal such as a tiger that could do very well in the wild will frequently give up that freedom and return to the safety of its cage and the certainty of free meals.

People are no different, even folks like us who claim to seek adventure. When faced with the squalid, confused reality of India, we spent our time searching for clean, well-lighted places. In Mysore, we unapologetically ate at Subway because the food was predictable—and therefore comforting. But by constantly seeking refuge *from* India, we had missed out *on* India, and that was a shame. If we could have found the requisite courage to let go of our desire for order, India instantly would have become more enjoyable.

En route to the Bangalore airport we passed a McDonalds, and the kids insisted that we stop. Our driver, who looked frighteningly similar to Osama Bin Laden, advised us to get the food to go because we were running late and traffic could be bad. The McDonalds didn't serve hamburgers, so we had sundaes and French fries. Joey collected garbage from the back seat of our car and put it in a bag. He handed it to our driver and said, "Would you mind throwing this away at the next garbage can?" Osama promptly rolled down his window and slam-dunked the garbage into the middle of the road!

At the Bangalore Airport we received an e-mail from Deniz in reply to our message about our struggles in India. Deniz wrote, "I am sorry to hear this. Not that the whole of one year-long journey is supposed to be equally nice and easy, though. The tougher places will also be an important part of the experience, I believe. The kids will value this tough India experience as much as the ones at the beautiful places. Maybe not right away but in the future they will."

I read his missive aloud to the kids, who listened silently and bobbled their heads.

CHAPTER 9

THAILAND

A Family Lost, a Family Found | *December 27, 2007– January 20, 2008*

*J*ill and I had been to Bangkok in 1993, and we recalled it as a loud, dirty city with crazy drivers, but, to our surprise, our cab ride from Bangkok's airport to our hotel in the Silom district was peaceful. The taxi had seat belts. When the driver wanted to change lanes, instead of blowing his horn, he used his turn signal. Bangkok is known for its terrible air pollution, but to us the air tasted like the air in Yellowstone.

Could Bangkok have changed this much in fourteen years? No. Our reality is shaped by recent memory, not distant memory, and our minds were measuring Bangkok not by our longtime home in Arizona, but by India, where we had spent the last few weeks. Compared with India, Bangkok was clean, polite, and efficient—a breath of fresh air.

When we arrived at our hotel we were greeted by the hotel clerk with the phrase *"Suwadee krap,"* which means "hello." Then he pointed to Tommy and said, "Suwadee krap, Mr. Harry Potter." Tom's hair had grown out from that horrible haircut in Turkey and he did look a little like Harry Potter. To Asian eyes, he must have looked exactly like Harry Potter, because the hotel staff asked him to pose for pictures.

Our hotel was comparable to a Holiday Inn, and we reveled in rediscovered luxury. When Jill entered the room, she took off her shoes and smiled as she wiggled her toes in the carpet. She excitedly showed me the hotel's clean white towels and then drew a bath with hot, clear water. I turned the air conditioner to its most frigid setting, laid my stinky self down on the soft bed, propped up my head with two feather pillows, and turned on cable TV.

The following afternoon as we ventured out into the heat, Jill and I found the Bangkok we remembered, a city where food vendors, beggars, and fortune tellers mingle with tourists in the crowded streets. At a 7-11 convenience store, we treated ourselves to huge Diet Cokes. A block farther, we found an entire street full of restaurants. The sign above one read, "New York Deli." We hadn't had a good deli sandwich since—well, since New York. Tommy bit into his microwaved tuna melt and began to scream. The cheese was scalding hot—and by the time we left the restaurant, his lip was starting to blister.

A newly built monorail took us from near our hotel to almost anywhere else in the city that we wanted to travel. To make up for the restrained Christmas, Jill and I gave each of the kids twenty dollars to spend. We all boarded the sky train to the Chatuchak Market, which is also known as the JJ Market. An open-air market, Chatuchak has more than fifteen thousand stalls set up in a maze of small narrow lanes and alleyways reminiscent of an Arabic souq.

Some two hundred thousand shoppers pass through the market every weekend. There were hundreds of stalls all selling the same things. Microsoft Office was available for eight dollars. Video games that retail in the United States for thirty dollars could be had for one dollar, and DVDs of first-run movies still in the theater could be found for two dollars. There was no attempt to hide that these were pirated copies. We talked it over with the kids about whether or not it was right to buy pirated software. We explained that the people who make the movies or write the programs for the games put in a lot of time and effort and because these were pirated, those workers wouldn't see any of the profits. We also explained that these programs might have viruses and might not run on their computers or game systems. But in the end we left the decision up to them.

As we walked through the market, I was in my usual place, in back of the family. As we moved through a narrow alley, I bent down to look at a small wood carving of a frog that makes a croaking sound when its back is rubbed by a wooden rod. When I looked up, the rest of the family had vanished. I walked for a block, looking down each lane as I passed, but I couldn't find them. I wandered around for over an hour, and still no luck.

I considered notifying the Thai police. They were well-armed and plentiful, but I don't speak Thai and wouldn't know what to say even if I did. My mind kept coming back to 1980s police shows I used to watch, where a concerned family member would explain to the police sergeant that his loved one was missing. The sergeant, tough but fair, would always say the same thing: "Dammit, I'd like to help you, but I can't list them as officially missing until they have been gone for at least twenty-four hours."

Was this really the law? Was it the law in Thailand? I had no idea.

At the lost-and-found office, I explained my predicament. They asked if my wife had a cell phone. She did, but it was in the hotel room. In any case, I didn't know the number. They asked if I had a business card for the hotel. I didn't. I knew the name—the Swiss Lodge. We looked in the directory but couldn't find the phone number. We then paged the family on the market's public address system. While waiting for my family to show up, I put a note on the bulletin board, instructing them to stay at the lost-and-found office and wait. When I described my family to a woman near the office, she said, "Oh—no problem. I see blonde woman with two boy."

"You mean two boys and a girl?" I asked

"No. Blonde woman two boy, one big, one little."

Until that moment, it had not occurred to me that the four of them might not be together. I realized that Jill might be assuming that a child not with her was with me. Bangkok is a city of 9 million souls, and a city famous for its sex trade. There really are a lot of perverts in Thailand. In fact, it is a place of pilgrimage for perverts. What would my precious little blonde seven-year-old be worth in such a place?

Fighting back a sense of horror, determined to keep my head, I found a map of the market and continued my search. Usually, the family picked a meeting place in case something like this ever occurred, but we had grown complacent and had forgotten to do so. I went everywhere that looked like a potential meeting point—exits, banks, ATMs—but I still didn't find them. I returned to the lost and found. My family was still not there, but the lady had found the number to our hotel. I called it. The clerk at the front desk hadn't seen my family but he said they could have walked by when he wasn't looking, so he connected me with our room. The phone rang and rang.

I made a second announcement on the loud speakers and waited. I then decided to search the crowded market stalls. I divided the market into quadrants and searched each one, alley by crowded alley. This took about an hour. By the time I came out, the stifling heat was beginning to ease and the lights of the market were on. It was no longer as easy to see detailed features as it was during the daytime, so I looked for people walking in groups of four who matched the general shape of my family. The darker it became, the less chance I had of finding them. I was beginning to panic. I took one more lap around the outside of the market and went back to the lost and found.

They were still not there, and the note I had left was untouched. Tom and Helen's words came back to me: "We left with three kids, and we are determined to come back with three." Here I was, in a far-off land, and the worst seemed to have happened. I felt nauseous, and no longer able to keep my head. I sat down and began to cry.

The same nice lady who had helped me before saw me crying and came over with her cell phone. I called the hotel again.

"Suwadee krap," I said to the hotel clerk. "This is Mr. Boesch."

"Suwadee krap, Mr. Boesch. Harry Potter here."

"How about his mother, brother, and sister?"

"All family here. You come here too."

When I arrived back at the Swiss Lodge, I was overjoyed to be reunited with the family, but Jill was angry with me. "Why didn't you just go to the sky train station? That was the obvious rendezvous point. We waited for you for over an hour," she said. Joey agreed with Jill, but to me it had not been obvious at all. I had all five sky train passes and, forgetting that we had given the kids their own cash, thought I had all the money.

The next night was New Year's Eve. Jill and I had planned on going out with Leith and Mel, an Australian couple we had met in our hotel, but given the drama of the previous day, we were reluctant. Their two boys joined our kids to watch a pirated DVD of *The Simpsons Movie.*

We gave Joey our cell phone number and made him do a practice call. We said we would call every half hour to check on them, and we had hotel business cards with us. On our way out the door, I said, "Joe, if we don't come back. . . ." He rolled his eyes and said, "I know, I know. Go to the front desk and have them call the embassy."

The four of us went to Patpong, Bangkok's red-light district. Touts approached with papers advertising "ping pong shows." Lots of "boy-girls" walked the streets. We saw several bad Thai Elvis Presley impersonators. Even more disturbing were the many overweight, balding, middle-aged Caucasian men wearing short pants, brown socks, and sandals—men who looked like me, in other words. They were walking hand in hand with beautiful twenty-year-old Thai women. I cringed at the sight.

The following morning we took a train for the city of Kanchanaburi, home to the famous *Bridge over the River Kwai* of World War II fame. Budget travel is an acquired skill, and after six months away from home, we were now much better at it than when we started. Rude people, dirty rooms, long lines, hard seats, lack of showers—none of these now frightened us in the least. Because we were no longer afraid of discomfort, we were less limited in our choices.

We had carefully planned everything in England, Tanzania, and France, but not anymore. Apart from our first night in a new country, we no longer had advance reservations. We made up our itinerary as we went along. In regard to Kanchanaburi, that meant we simply went to the train station, bought tickets, and headed north.

In addition to the famous bridge, Kanchanaburi is known for the Tiger Temple. This Buddhist-run sanctuary is a place where orphaned tigers are raised in captivity. The tigers spend most of the day sleeping and have become habituated to people, which allows for close contact with the animals.

As we stood in a long line waiting to get a picture with the tigers, the lama in charge of the sanctuary walked by. When he caught site of Cami, he smiled and took her by the hand past the front of the line and right up to the very biggest tiger. The beast was stretched out on his back like a snoozing housecat. The lama plopped Cami right on its belly. Of all the photos we published on our website, this drew the most criticism. People wrote to ask, "Are you crazy? One swipe of that tiger's paw and she could have been dead."

I responded by writing back, "Everyone else was doing it"—a lame explanation on its surface and one that never worked with my parents and doesn't work with me. As a scientist, I would say that having seen tens of people safely go in front of us, the probability of a mauling decreased with each person that safely returned.

We visited a shop on the banks of the River Kwai. Behind the main display case was a large painting of the Thai King—a.k.a. Bhumibol Adulyadej, a.k.a. Rama IX. The shop owner's English was good, so I asked him how he felt about the king. "My king loves Thailand and cares about people like me personally. He is a great man and can even make it rain if my king wants to, especially during the rainy season," he said with a smile.

Born in Cambridge, Massachusetts, and educated in Switzerland at a time when the Thai monarchy was languishing, Bhumibol was never supposed to be king. That honor was intended for his older brother Mahidol. When his brother was shot in the head under mysterious circumstances in 1946, Bhumibol assumed the throne and has been there ever since. During those sixty-plus years on the throne (the longest reign of any king in recorded history), Thailand has changed from a Third World backwater into a developed country. Per capita income for the average Thai has increased forty-fold.

Thailand has a democratically elected government. As a Constitutional Monarch, King Bhumibol has only three "rights": the right to encourage, the right to warn, and the right to be consulted. A wise king would want no more.

The king is reluctant to intervene publicly and typically does so only at the last hour. In 1992, with tanks in the streets and his country on the brink of civil war, King Bhumibol called leaders from warring factions into his office. With the men kneeling in front of him and TV cameras rolling, he reprimanded both men the way a principal would two misbehaving teens. This public castigation was enough. Both men left Thailand in disgrace and combatants on both sides went home. The simmering civil war simply stopped.

One month before we arrived, the Thai military had seized power from the civilian government. In most countries, the takeover would be a big deal, but this was Thailand's seventeenth bloodless coup in the last sixty years. Thus far, the king had made no comment.

Thailand has a Lese Majesty law, which means than anyone found criticizing the Royal family can be charged with a crime. (In his annual speech in 2005, Bhumibol encouraged people not to take this law seriously.) I motioned the owner toward a more private part of the shop. "What do you really think of the king," I asked.

"I told you already," he replied. "How about the queen?" I asked. "Don't like her at all," he replied. "How about the prince?" (Bhumibol's son has a reputation as a brute.) "I like him even less. He is horrible. I worry what will become of the country when my king dies."

"What do you like so much about the king?" I asked.

"He lives modestly. He spends his days listening to average Thais like me. He takes our concerns seriously and tries to help us. He runs a big charity, and every December he gives a speech in which he compares the efficiency of his charity with the wastefulness of the government. He is typically shown wearing a camera around his neck, which he uses to photograph his subjects because he loves them the way a good father loves his children."

He continued, "My king is also a good saxophonist and an excellent sailor. He is a devout Buddhist and was even a monk for a while."

Bhumibol's favorite color is yellow. Every Monday, Thais wear yellow shirts to show their devotion, and so we wore yellow on our flight from Bangkok to Chiang Mai in northern Thailand, near the borders with Laos and Burma.

As we stood in line to check into our hotel, a Japanese couple was in front of us. They took note of Tommy and asked if they could take the usual "Harry Potter" picture. We were happy to oblige. When they checked in, they conversed with the Thai clerk in English. This didn't seem right. It seemed as though there should be some common Asian language, but there wasn't. Their alphabets weren't even similar. Just like everywhere else we had been, English was the default language.

A friend had arranged for us to have a driver meet us. His name was Ache, and we fondly referred to his white van as the Achemobile. Every morning, Ache showed up at our hotel to drive us around the hills of northern Thailand. On the third day, he drove us along the banks of the Mekong River to a place known as "the Golden Triangle," so named due to its fame for heroin production. It was time for Ache to show off his English: "Burma oba dare. Laos oba dare. You like Burma?" he asked as we approached a bridge.

We responded with our best Indian head bobble. We hadn't given much thought to whether we fancied Burma or not. But here was this half-mile bridge, and on the other side was Burma—literally right "oba dare." Ache explained that he couldn't drive in Burma because the Achemobile wasn't suited to the task. In Thailand driving is done on the left, in Burma on the right. He also demanded to be paid in cash for the previous three days before we crossed the bridge (roughly $150 U.S.). I argued with him about this, and he began to get upset.

We found an interpreter who explained to us that on two separate occasions, Ache had dropped tourists off at the border with a promise to wait for them, and they never returned, leaving him unpaid for his services. We pointed out that our luggage was in his van and that we had no intention of moving to Burma, but this did not convince him. We paid him and headed for the bridge.

As we stood in line to cross, Jill grabbed my sleeve and pulled me off to the side. "Look," she said, "the only reason to pay to cross this bridge is to be able to say we have been to Burma, and we haven't gone anywhere just for that reason yet. I vote we don't go." We had binoculars with us and could see what was on the other side of the bridge—a bunch of stalls selling junk. It didn't look any different from where we were standing, except there were no 7-11 stores.

When I suggested we leave the decision of whether or not to go to Burma up to the kids, Jill agreed. We explained to them that the Burmese government has a terrible record of human rights abuses, and that the fee we would be paying to enter Burma would go to this government. On the other hand, we said, this would be our only chance to visit Burma, and the best way to form an opinion about a place is to go and see it for yourself. Jill and I told the kids to make a decision and then we walked away. We were proud of the ten-minute discussion that ensued before the kids reached a consensus.

We had read about a Buddhist monastery where the monks were willing to talk with visitors as long as women guests dressed modestly and refrained from touching the monks. We asked Ache to take us there.

Virtually every Thai male spends some time as a monk, typically after graduation from high school. The boys have their head shaved and begin as novices. Some stay all their lives, some for only a few months. Ache himself had been a monk for two years, and he was delighted to take us.

We met Tom and Jerry, two monks from Cambodia who were studying in Thailand. The kids were taken aback when Jerry told them that they don't believe in God.

"Who do you pray to?" Tommy asked.

"Our prayer is within, not without," said Tom.

Cami asked, "How do you get your food?"

Jerry, whose English was better than Tom's, replied, "Every morning shortly after sunrise, we walk around to the houses in town with our alms bowls that hopefully will be filled with enough food to get us through the day. People give to us in order to make merit. We eat breakfast and lunch but do not eat after noon."

"Is it like Halloween where some people give lots of good candy and other people give junky candy?" Cami asked.

"I don't know about Halloween, but some food is better than others."

"What do you do the rest of the day?" I asked.

"Study, meditate, watch TV."

"TV?" I asked, surprised.

"Cable," he replied.

The next afternoon, we saw a monk wearing traditional robes buying sour cream and onion Pringles in a 7-11. "I wonder if they know about that back at the monastery," Joe asked.

From Chiang Mai we drove to Chiang Rai, a less-visited area of northern Thailand. There, we decided to take a boat trip down the Mekong River. Ache pointed to a few boat captains lying on some rocks near the river, their boats tied up nearby. I noticed a pungent aroma as I walked toward them. Their speech was slurred and their pupils small. There was no way I was going to put my family's lives in the hands of these opium smokers. The river was shallow in spots, and the boats were like big wooden canoes, only with old diesel motors and props that stuck out fifteen feet from the back of a long metal bar on each boat. These were the famous long-tailed boats of Thailand. We located an old one-armed, chain-smoking boat pilot who was not stoned, and he took us for a great ride.

Ache drove us back to Chiang Mai. I planned on tipping him but wanted to give him more than just money. He had been so nice to us and he was a good, safe driver—but his English was terrible. We got by mostly with pantomime and a phrase book. If he wanted to continue doing business, better English would have been a big help. So I had him take us to a bookstore where I looked and looked for Thai-to-English CDs (the Achemobile had a CD player), but I couldn't find any.

From Chiang Mai we flew south to Railay Beach in Thailand's Krabi province. Krabi had been largely spared damage by the tsunami of 2004, but places nearby had not. The five of us crowded into one room, meant for two people, at a rate of $180 per night. This was our second "resort experience" of the entire year. As in Zanzibar, we found that after one day on the beach we were bored, but we had prepaid reservations for a week.

Railay Beach is well known for rock climbing. The boys had climbed a lot on climbing walls, but this was their first time on real rock. Tommy was near the top of a particularly difficult climb when we heard a voice that didn't sound like Tommy. In the tree above him was a little green monkey who was laughing while urinating right on Tommy's head.

The next day was Tommy's tenth birthday. We let the staff at the hotel know. They recommended we hire a long-tailed boat and go snorkeling. The water was crystal clear and loaded with fish and sea urchins. Suddenly Tommy jerked off his mask and began screaming and pointing to his left shoulder. We got back into the boat, and I examined him. After a few minutes, Tommy began developing blisters on his shoulder to match those still on his lip. Tommy had been stung by a jellyfish.

Jellyfish venom is known as a heat-labile toxin, which means that if you apply heat to the place where you were stung, the venom will be neutralized and the pain will recede. The treatment for any jellyfish sting is immersion in hot water. We were on a small wooden boat a long way from civilization and there was no hot water to be found.

"I'll pee on it for you, Tommy," Joey offered. "I have to go anyway."

It wasn't so much what Joe said as it was the way in which he said it. His offer was selfless and not meant to demean Tommy. This wasn't the alpha dog pissing on the new member of the pack, but a kind gesture from a concerned older brother who sincerely wanted Tommy to enjoy his birthday. We were a different family now from when we left the United States. Our seven months of constant contact had brought us closer together, and Joe's offer to urinate on his brother was a bizarre yet touching symbol of this closeness.

"I'll pee on it myself," Tommy said.

Tommy turned his back to the rest of us, pulled down his swimsuit, and took aim. It is simple for a male to urinate on his own shoulder while lying supine. (Guys, if you don't believe me, try this yourself at home.) Standing is another story. This requires accuracy, a vertical stream strong enough to defy gravity and (in the present case) the ability to correct for a rocking boat. Tommy's attempt wasn't even close and the warm, golden shower of urine meant to soothe his stinging shoulder fell feebly into the Andaman Sea.

"Too bad that monkey from yesterday isn't here, Tommy," Joey commented. "He could have peed on it for you."

Tommy didn't let the jellyfish sting ruin his birthday. He got back in the water and found a huge black eel poking its head out from under a rock.

We noticed some fellow snorkelers who looked like some of the whore chasers we had seen back in Bangkok, only these guys were wearing Speedos instead of brown socks. Joe pointed out the eel to them. They replied in a thick German accent, "Yah, eel. Very dangerous." The Germans returned with a spear gun with the intent of shooting the eel. It was clear they didn't know what they were doing, so we retreated to the safety of the boat and the eel retreated under the rock until the Germans gave up and swam away.

That night we had dinner at the resort's restaurant, where the staff had prepared a special cake that bore this inscription: "Happy Birthday, Harry Potter."

CHAPTER 10

JAPAN

Cami's Broken Leg | *January 21–29, 2008*

*J*ill and I didn't want to go to Japan. We never stuck a pin in Japan in our map on the wall, and we never bothered to check the weather in the world weather guide. We had preconceived ideas that Japan was crowded and expensive. Furthermore, after two months in Asia, we were ready to head to Australia and speak English again.

Japan was all Joe's idea. Joe had a friend who had traveled to Japan, and whenever we discussed our itinerary Joe would bring it up. At an English bookstore in Venice, Italy, we bought two guidebooks on Japan and told Joe that if he planned the trip we would go. We had yet to purchase tickets for the second half of our trip, so adding another country was still possible. Jill and I both thought that Joe would lose interest and that would be the end of it. Instead, two days later he gave us the book back. In it, he had highlighted Sumo matches, the Toshiba factory tour, and skiing in Nagano. He also planned our train routes.

After landing in Osaka we hopped aboard an express train to Kyoto that departed at 09:23, right on time. We arrived in Kyoto's central station on a cold, misty day. As we wheeled our luggage a half-mile to our hotel, we walked past row upon row of bicycles—none of them locked.

Before leaving the United States, we had decided that we would always begin our conversations in the native tongue of the country we were visiting. We would continue in that language as far as possible before defaulting back to English. To do otherwise would have been rude.

I speak Italian and Spanish well enough to get by, and I even remember a little French from Mr. Azzara's high school class. No one in the family speaks Swahili or Turkish, but both of these languages use something similar to the Roman alphabet. In a pinch, we would pull out our dictionary and look up the necessary word in order to be understood.

Japan had no written language until A.D. 400, when they began to import and adapt Chinese characters (*kanji*) by way of the Korean Peninsula. Some Chinese characters stand for words, others stand for sounds. The Japanese continued to blend and modify these and also added components of English. The result is four separate alphabets: hiragana, katakana, kanji, and romaji. Modern Japanese writing is a seamless blend of these four alphabets.

It requires great dedication for a Westerner to learn to read and write Japanese, so we tried to learn to speak it instead. We bought Japanese language tapes and listened to them over and over. This was slow going for all of us except Tommy, who has a real ear for languages. At our hotel, Tommy walked up to the three twenty-something female desk clerks, gave a bow, and said, "*Konnichiwa.*"

"Oh look," said one of the clerks. "Little Harry Potter speak Japanese."

We introduced the whole family, and the clerks took time to make us feel welcome and teach us a few more Japanese words. They took a special interest in Cami, even calling over several co-workers to look at her blonde hair.

Once in our hotel room, I grabbed the newspaper and headed for the toilet. The bathroom was smaller than the one on the airplane, and there was no toilet paper. A symbol for a sprayer and a bunch of buttons was on a handle near the heated toilet seat. I pushed one and a chrome handle emerged right under "ground zero" and began a warm and very vigorous spray. Wow—welcome to Japan! With a push of a button I adjusted the force of the spray as well as the temperature of the water (I recommend hot).

High-tech gadgetry is everywhere in Japan, not just on toilets. On our first night we went to a five-story electronics store, where I replaced the camera that had been stolen in Italy. The highlight of the evening was the massage chair. I remember massage chairs from the 1980s that vibrated like a "magic fingers bed," and when they finished you were more likely to feel seasick than relaxed. These Japanese chairs squeeze your arms and legs like a blood pressure cuff and then knead your muscles, providing a vigorous massage from your toes up to your neck. After thirty minutes in the massage chairs—and tired from our overnight flight—we were soon ready for bed.

The following morning we woke up early and took the subway to Kiyomazu Temple. A Buddhist temple in Eastern Kyoto originally built in 798, the wooden structure was reconstructed in the 1600s entirely without nails. Kiyomazu means "pure water" because the temple itself is constructed around a waterfall. A platform extends outward from the main temple and at one time it was believed that if you survived the forty-foot jump off the stage, whatever you wished for would come true. Even though 85 percent of the jumpers survived, the practice is now illegal.

From there we took a bus to the Kyoto Tower. By now the sun had set, and from the top of the four-hundred-foot tower we could look out and see brand-new buildings and century-old temples. The kids' favorite thing to look at from the top of the tower was a six-story driving range, where each stall was filled with a golfer.

With 890 people per square mile, Japan was the most densely populated country we had visited. (The United States is eighty people per square mile; the world average is 117.) Kyoto was a crowded place, but it didn't feel crowded. The city felt tranquil. That is an unusual adjective to describe a big city, but the decorum in Kyoto was surreal: No littering, no line cutting, no rude talk, train patrons wait single file to board the trains, trains run on time, and everyone gets where they need to go.

Kyoto is a fashion-conscious city where most men wear suits and women wear skirts and boots, all in dark winter colors. The only fashion accessory that was out of place was the periwinkle-hued surgical masks worn by many to prevent the spread of influenza.

We were struck by the great pride the Japanese take in their work. Jobs that we consider menial—convenience store clerk, cab driver, train ticket checker, McDonald's nugget cooker—are all performed with great dignity. You don't need to speak Japanese to figure it out either; you can tell it by the body language and dress of the workers.

After three days in Kyoto, we took the train to Nagano, site of the 1998 Winter Olympics. Cami had only skied once before and was in need of a lesson. Our options were a group lesson in Japanese ($30) or a private lesson in English ($125). I encouraged the Japanese group lesson and tried to sell it based on cultural reasons, but having lived with my parsimony for more than eight months, no one in the family believed that explanation. We opted for the English lesson.

Cami's instructor was a nice New Zealander who told her to "look out for sea lions." This does not refer to the large, stinky marine mammals but to the Japanese teen snowboarders that lie on the slopes and text message each other instead of boarding. Cami's teacher said that some of them sit there all day and only ski down once.

We expected big crowds and high prices but were pleasantly surprised. Lift tickets were about thirty-five dollars for adults and twenty dollars for kids, equipment rental was reasonable, and chairlift lines were short. Our first day skiing was bitterly cold. High winds forced the closure of all the chairlifts higher on the mountain. The following day, the weather improved. Here is Jill's description:

I decided to ski with Cami on her second day. She had done well in her lesson, but wasn't good enough to keep up with the boys.

Around 1:30, Tommy caught up with us and led us to a different, but still easy part of the mountain. Near the bottom, Cami fell. It wasn't a hard crash, not a big head-over-heels wipe out, just a run-of-the-mill fall. I tried helping her up but every time she would attempt to bear weight on her left leg she would scream.

I eventually was able to flag down the ski patrol. He didn't speak English, but could see that we were having problems, so he picked Cami up and skied the remaining quarter mile to the first aid hut while I skied behind them lugging Cami's skis, Tommy was nowhere to be found.

A young woman approached us in the first aid tent. "Kunnichiwa," I said. "Hello," she replied. I was excited that someone spoke English, but I think "hello" was the only word she knew how to say. She got a pen and paper and neatly printed the word "husband?" I pointed to the top of the mountain and she went to get a microphone so that I could page David on the loudspeaker.

The ski patrol guy who had carried Cami down was trying to remove her boot, and each time he would pull, she would cry out in pain. It was awful. I have never heard her scream like that before. I was so relieved when they finally got the boot off.

Cami must have seen the concern on my face. "Is this a trip ender?" she asked as she began to cry.

"Why honey?" I replied "Do you want to go home?"

"Well, I miss the dogs," she said, "but I don't want to miss out on the rest of the world."

Tears came to my eyes when she said that because right up until then, I had always felt that Cami was the one member of the family who would rather have stayed home. Hearing her say those words at that time lifted my heart. What a brave little girl.

David didn't answer his page.

The woman in the tent wrote "main lodge, husband" on a piece of paper and pointed to the snow mobile. Cami was terrified that I was going to leave her, but I had to go find David.

On the way there, I saw Tommy and Joe. I tapped the snow mobile driver on the shoulder and pointed to them. He drove up.

"Cool snow mobile," Joe said.

"Thanks." I replied. "I think your sister broke her leg. I'm heading to the main lodge in hopes of finding dad."

"OK," Tommy replied. "We'll go on this run one more time and then meet you there."

"No. Go there now, hand in your skis and help look for dad."

It was about a 10-minute ride and as soon as we pulled up, David was walking out.

A few minutes later, Cami arrived on the back of a second snowmobile. I caught up with her in the first aid tent and examined her leg. She was tender over the middle part of her tibia (the big bone in her lower leg). She was also unable to bear weight on that leg. Those two facts made it likely that she had broken her leg, but a bruise was also possible.

The first aid worker placed Cami's leg in a splint. We considered leaving that on for a few days to see how she did, but the treatments for the two conditions are different. It's okay to walk on a bruised leg, but not on a fracture. Cami needed an X-ray, and she needed it right away. It was 2 p.m. We had a train to catch at 3:49, and Mr. Kato, the man who had rented us his cabin, was coming to take us to the train station. When Mr. Kato arrived, we asked him to take us to the hospital instead.

Even though Japan is a modern country we were concerned about the type of care Cami would receive. Japan has the highest per capita number of CT scanners in the entire world. Japanese doctors are paid based on how much they charge, so they tend to over-order expensive tests and to over-prescribe medications. Nationalized health care leads to long waits for everything except dire emergencies. The phrase used in Japan is "a three-hour wait for a three-minute contact." Given that, we were resigned to another day in Nagano, knowing there was no way we would make our train. The boys were already asking if they could ski again the next day.

When we arrived at the hospital, we were greeted by three young women who, despite the snow outside, were dressed identically in light blue cotton smocks. With a smile, a bow, and a "konnichiwa," they brought a wheelchair out for Cami, and we walked through the front door and into the lobby. Suddenly we realized that we had done something horribly wrong. These polite young women who were so gracious to Cami were now very upset with us. They yelled at us and pointed at the floor—no, not at the floor, but at our shoes. "Sumimasen," Tommy said, apologizing as we took of our shoes and put on slippers.

The young women were now smiling and bowing again. We reunited with Cami in an exam room, where her completed X-ray was already up on two view boxes. The box near me displayed the front-to-back view of Cami's leg and it was normal. My hopes were raised. Then I looked over at Jill, who was sadly shaking her head. In medical school one of the first things you learn about radiology is that one view means nothing. An X-ray is not normal until it is normal from two separate views. The X-ray in front of Jill, the one taken from the side, showed what the X-ray in front of me did not—a broken leg.

In walked Dr. Shintani Tsuyishi, the doctor on duty and the owner of the clinic. He carefully examined Cami's leg. Then he informed us that Cami did indeed have a fracture of her tibia. The good news was that the break was in a good position and Cami would not need an operation.

As the doctor gently applied the cast to Cami's leg, I told him that I too was a physician, and we traded a few stories. When he finished applying the cast, he told me about his brand-new 32 detector CT scan machine. He had saved five years to buy it and was clearly very proud. He showed me some images from his CT files of a bruised lung (snowboarding), lacerated spleen (snowboarding), and dislocated hip (snowboarding). "Snowboarding very good for business," he said, laughing.

The bill came to $420 for everything—diagnosis, casting, two sets of X-rays—and all that took just 40 minutes. It was now 3:10, and we had time to get Cami a chicken nugget Happy Meal before our train departed at 3:49. As we waited for the train to arrive, I dug out our insurance information and under "excluded injuries" the first one listed was "injuries resulting from snow skiing."

On the train, Joe asked, "Is this a trip ender?"

"Your first concern should be your sister's welfare," I said angrily.

Dr. Tsuyishi did not have crutches in her size, so I had to carry Cami. As her dad, I welcomed the opportunity to carry my little girl, but it did slow us down. We had five days left in Japan. Our next stop was Tsuruga City, where we planned to meet a friend's brother who was in Japan teaching English.

Tsuruga City was only two hours from Nagano but required three train changes to get there. Trains in Japan don't stop for very long, so when our train would come to a halt, we would pile some of the bags onto the platform, leave Tommy to wait with them, and then go back to get Cami and the rest of the bags. It was snowing, and the platforms were slick. A second slip and fall could have made Cami's fracture worse.

We arrived in Tsuruga late at night, and we hadn't had any dinner. The hotel restaurant was closed and all we had left to eat was one box of curry noodles. After India I was the only one in the family who would still eat curry, but all I had to eat them with was a toothbrush. I began heating water for the noodles and by the time it was boiling Jill returned with four ice creams, two cold beers, two Cokes, and a pile of hot chicken nuggets.

"Where did you get all those?" I asked.

"The vending machine."

"How many vending machines do they have?"

"Only one, but it is really cool."

In addition to cool vending machines, Japan has many convenience stores, including 7-11. The kids enjoyed stopping in these stores every day for dollar snacks and "America Dogs," which we know in the United States as corn dogs.

I managed to get Internet access (in this hotel it was done through the electrical power cord, not wirelessly or via a separate phone connection), I e-mailed two friends—an orthopedist and a pediatrician—to describe Cami's fracture. I wanted their input on how long and in what fashion Cami would need to be casted. I also sent an e-mail to all of our friends about Cami's fracture. I said that our trip was in jeopardy and asked them to send words of encouragement (as well as any dog pictures) to raise Cami's spirits.

Here is Cami's journal entry from the day she broke her leg:

Today we went skiing. My mom desided she was going to go skiing our last day there. My mom hasn't skied in 13 years. My mom had a very fun time skiing. We only went on 2 runs. One was a little bit steeper than the other one I usually was on the most. The other run had some jumps on it. Tommy went off one of the jumps but he did not stick the jump. I had lots of fun skiing today.

In addition to neglecting to mention her broken leg, Cami insisted that I not put any pictures of her broken leg on the website. She was embarrassed, as though she had done something wrong.

The next day was wonderful. We had breakfast in our robes in the hotel and then met Paul, our friend's brother. He and his girlfriend, Lisa, had both taken time off after college to teach English in Japan. They were nearing the end of their two-year commitment.

We began the day at a Japanese cultural center where the kids learned calligraphy from Paul's good friend, a delightful ninety-three-year-old Japanese woman named Atago-sensei. She had coupons for the Japanese equivalent of a Denny's, and she wanted to take us to lunch. Joe rode to the restaurant in the front passenger seat of her car, but after lunch, he didn't want to ride back. I told him that she was just a sweet little old lady and that riding with her was a tremendous chance to learn Japanese culture. He said, "I know that, Dad, but she is a terrible driver—even worse than you—and we had a couple of close calls on the way."

Paul and Lisa took us to the seven lakes region of Tsuruga, a beautiful snow-covered area with a view of the Sea of Japan. When we parked the car, Joey and Tommy started a snowball fight with Paul. I had grown tired of horseplay, but to Paul this was new, and it provided a nice outlet for the boys' rowdy energy.

Next, Joe pushed Tommy into a phone booth. The door to the phone booth opened outward and Joe leaned against the door, keeping it closed while he built up snow outside so that Tommy couldn't escape. Tommy began knocking on the glass and yelling for help. We thought he was kidding, but Joey had done a good job of barricading him in. After a lot of digging, we finally got the door open. Tommy said, "I'm glad you got me out. I thought I was going to have to call "1-1-9."

"You mean 9-1-1," Jill replied.

"No, 1-1-9," Tommy said, showing us a sign with the emergency number in Japan: 1-1-9.

That night, Paul took Tommy, Joey, and me to a local gymnasium to watch some men practice the Japanese sword-drawing martial art known as *Laido*. The gym had a wooden floor and was very cold. We watched in silence as these men drew their metal swords from the sheaths and practiced various moves, many of which took place from the kneeling position. The swordsmen clearly were not used to visitors and the oldest of the group kept sneering at us as he would draw his sword. After a time, one of the masters came over and asked if we had any questions. He patiently explained the history of Laido and demonstrated how he could defeat up to eight combatants at a time while still on his knees.

The following morning, when we boarded the train to Kyoto, big flakes of snow were falling. Japanese schoolgirls dressed in short, green-and-black-checked skirts and white dress shirts texted and giggled as the train took us slowly through the mountains from town to town. The towns themselves were tightly packed with apartments, but the countryside in between was pristine.

Here is Cami's description:

Today we went on a butiful train ride. We passed a little town covered in snow. We saw some crops in the town the crops were covered in snow. The train was 1 and a half hours. We saw lots of prity mountains along the way. We went thru lots of tunnels to get thru the mountins. We were heading to a city still in Japan. It was cold Kyoto. I was watching my IPod part of the time then I stoped watching my IPOD and I looked out the window the rest of the way. it was a nice train ride.

When I carried Cami into our same Kyoto hotel, the same three desk clerks we had met the first day were on duty. When they saw Cami's cast, their mouths dropped open. They quickly covered them and their eyes widened (looking like three "speak no evil" monkeys). We explained what happened, and the young women quickly ran and got some candy for Cami.

To further cheer up Cami, Jill and I carried her half a mile to a "glamour" photo studio where two stern Japanese ladies spent forty-five minutes applying white makeup and then dressing Cami in a *maiko* outfit. There were a limited number of poses she could do because of her cast, and at first Cami was embarrassed, but after a few photos, she grew to like the posing.

Maiko are geisha in training. I didn't know much about geisha so I asked the women applying Cami's makeup. They explained that the literal translation of geisha is "performing artist" and that this can include anything from pouring tea to prostitution. There are only about one thousand left in the entire country, and their numbers are dwindling. If we wanted to see an actual geisha they recommended a trip to a section of Kyoto known as the Guion District. We should arrive near dusk because that is when the geisha are most active; if we were lucky we might see one entering or leaving a teahouse. We began our geisha safari in the rain at 6 p.m. We walked through the entire Guion District. We got wet, we got lost, we bought some souvenirs—but we never did "bag" a geisha.

When we returned to the hotel I had e-mails from the pediatrician and the orthopedist. The pediatrician recommended six weeks in a long cast and two weeks in a short cast, with delayed weight bearing. He also admonished us to take this fracture seriously, as complications can develop. The orthopedist recommended two weeks in a long cast and two weeks in a short cast. He also said that he had a friend who is a pediatric orthopedist in Brisbane, Australia—our next stop—who would be happy to change Cami's cast.

The recommendations may sound similar, but from a practical point of view they were greatly different. The pediatrician's recommendation (and he is an excellent pediatrician) meant that I would have to carry Cami until we were two weeks into New Zealand, and that she would be in a cast until we reached Argentina. Furthermore, because muscles tend to atrophy when immobilized, Cami would likely be limping until we returned home in May. The orthopedist's recommendation (and he is an excellent orthopedist) meant that she could walk a few steps, within a week, and could be walking short distances within two more weeks.

Given that all of our plans in Australia and New Zealand were centered around outdoor activity, the difference between the two recommendations was the difference between continuing the trip and going home. Weight bearing was important because if Cami could walk, I could carry suitcases instead of her.

After much discussion, we decided to continue the trip. We called the airline to let them know about Cami's injury, and they kept the seat next to her open, so she could elevate her leg. When we arrived at the airport, we were escorted to the front of a long ticket line and then to the front of the line for passport control. We were grateful for the consideration, but none of us wanted to leave Japan. We wanted to complete the itinerary Joe had set out for us: see a Sumo match, see Mount Fuji, take a factory tour, and see Tokyo—but it was more than that. There was just so much more to learn.

Japan is monocultural, with ethnic Japanese comprising 99 percent of the population, and Japan is unique. From the moment we arrived we found Japan to be beautiful, safe, and polite. Japan drew us in, fascinated us, from high-tech toilets to the geishas to the eight-hundred-year-old temples. The more we learned, the more we wanted to learn. As our curiosity snowballed we began to notice contradictions between what we saw in person and what we knew from history. Joe in particular could not reconcile the grace we noticed in the Japanese people with their wartime brutality in the previous century. As his teacher, I was happy he noticed and happy to point out that Japan was not alone in this regard.

As we sat in Osaka's Kansai Airport waiting for our flight to Brisbane, Australia, we all wished we could have stayed longer. On the other hand, we knew our month in Australia would be easy, and we looked forward to that.

CHAPTER 11

AUSTRALIA

Sex Education in an RV | *January 31–February 27, 2008*

*O*f all the foreign languages we tried to learn, Australian was the simplest. Australians speak a variation of English that we found easy to master.

For words of two syllables or more, they simply shorten the second syllable and replace it with "ie."

Here are some examples:

breakfast = "brekkie"
barbecue = "barbie"
Sponge Bob = "Spongie"

We made up a few of our own:

postcards = "posties"
cell phone = "cellie"
prostate = "prostie"

As we landed in each country, we followed the same routine. After making our way through passport control and customs, we would find an ATM, locate a new SIM card for the cell phone, obtain a local map, and then arrange transportation to our accommodations. The kids had learned to expect a two-hour wait, but in Brisbane, where we spoke the language, the whole process took a mere forty-five minutes.

Our eleven-hour flight south took us from winter in Japan to summer in Australia, where it was 40 degrees warmer—the miracle of air travel. Our first stop was Caloundra, a little beach town on Australia's sunshine coast where we planned to learn how to surf.

As luck would have it, the weather had changed from rainy to clear the morning we arrived and summer break had just ended, so the beaches went from rainy and crowded to sunny and empty literally overnight. We were stoked. Long surfboards are the easiest to stand up on, so we rented three of the longest we could find. We also bought new swimsuits and surfing shirts ("rashies") to prevent chafing.

To me, growing up in St. Louis, Missouri, far from any ocean, surfing looked like the coolest of all sports. It also looked impossible. If the boys and I were to have any chance of success we needed lessons. I signed the three of us up with Bowie, a surfing coach we found in the local newspaper. He was nineteen years old, loved fast cars, and had long, sun-bleached hair.

"The waves here aren't as pumping as the Gold Coast," Bowie said. "They are usually combers, perfect for beginners, although today is a bit mushberger." The boys and I nodded. Bowie was a good teacher. He spent time explaining wave hydraulics and riptides. He also took pride in keeping us safe. "You kooks don't want to get rag-dolled on your first day," he said. We certainly did not.

The slacker-dude stereotype associated with surfing greatly underestimates the athleticism required for the sport. From beginner to expert, the initial move of surfing is the same. It is known as a "drop in," and it requires quickly popping up from a prone position to a standing position at just the right time, a relatively simple move provided you have the requisite strength, balance, and hip flexibility. With the sense of urgency you would expect from a forty-five-year-old who realizes this is his first and best chance to surf, I listened to every word Bowie said. I even brought the board back to our apartment to practice in front of the TV.

Joe and Tom didn't practice at all, yet they both got the hang of surfing. Despite three full days of effort (much of it done while the rest of the family was still in bed), I never did successfully stand up and ride a wave. While the boys surfed and I got chafed to the point of bleeding (below my rashie, in the most awful place imaginable), Jill and Cami spent long, boring days at the apartment. Here is how Cami spent a typical day:

Today I watched a movie. For brecfist we had pancakes with sirup. I watched nanny micfy agin. The boys went serfing today. Mom and I were going to get our heir cut but the girl got sick so we had to wait for four hours until we got our hair cut. I had a fun day. I liked my hair cut.

Ten days after Cami broke her leg, we went to see Dr. McGuire, my friend's colleague at Mater Children's Hospital in Brisbane. He examined the X-rays from Japan, removed Cami's long cast, and applied a short one with extra support in the heel so that Cami could put weight on it. The cast was then cut down both sides so that I could remove it.

"What is called for now is judgment," Dr. McGuire said. "She can begin partial weight bearing as soon as she can do so comfortably and then after a week if she is no longer limping you can remove the cast altogether. Two weeks after that, if she is still not limping she can resume usual activity."

Australia has a lot in common with the American West, with plenty of good roads and a lot of wide-open spaces. Despite some of the logistical issues, we had enjoyed our RV experience in the United States, and Australia seemed like an ideal place to try it again. We rented a camper this time, instead of a trailer. (A camper is one big self-powered unit; a trailer is pulled by another vehicle.) Our 29-foot-long, 11-½-foot-high Winnebago allegedly was big enough to sleep five. The interior was covered with brown paneling circa 1978. The words "leisure seeker" were painted in cursive near the roof on the passenger side. After we picked up the camper in Brisbane, we had two weeks to drive 1,051 miles to Melbourne. I loaded Tim, our GPS, with maps of Australia, and he came up with three options: Continue down the beach through Sydney, head west through the desert, or take the sparsely populated middle route known as the New England Highway. All the routes would be beautiful, but the experience in each would be quite different.

We went to Byron Bay to think it over. Byron Bay is the easternmost point in Australia. Here, an historic white lighthouse looks out over a pristine beach where dolphins played in the waves next to surfers. To the west are rain forests and macadamia nut plantations. The town itself has a laid-back vibe with sidewalk cafes, bars, pizza parlors, and surf shops.

We drove through town twice, but there was no place to park. Already, the Winnebago felt like a mistake. The difference between a camper and a trailer may not seem like much, but in our circumstances it was huge. The camper was our only source of transportation, so whenever we wanted to move we had to remove it from its hookups. Then we had to drive it. Ours had a transmission that could be either automatic or manual, but in both cases it accelerated slowly and things were constantly crashing off the shelves. It was hard to park. Worst of all, the camper meant we were always together.

Even though by this time in the trip we were getting along well, having five people together—one of whom can't walk—in the rain in a twenty-nine-foot cabin is not a good idea. We talked about returning the camper and switching to a car, but the rental had cost two thousand dollars for two weeks plus the four hundred dollars extra for the upgraded insurance policy that covered everything but "overhead damage"—and the cost was completely nonrefundable.

Jill backed the Winnebago into a parking spot on a side street half a mile from downtown. We covered Cami's blue cast with a plastic bag and I carried her through the rain to a second-hand store. There we bought Tom and Joe bicycles so that they could go from the trailer park into town.

After two mellow days in Byron Bay, we unhooked our septic tank and programmed our route into Tim. A new family was pulling in to our right, so I turned left and drove slowly past the community barbecue. A tree extended over the middle of the road. I kept driving. There was a crash. I thought something had fallen off the shelf, but now the camper seemed to be stuck. Jill screamed for me to stop. We got out to look.

A large hole was smashed near the "leisure seeker" logo, the awning was torn asunder and dangling by a solitary screw. The camper remained wedged under a huge branch, which rested on the roof. It was impossible to move it further.

Peter, the park maintenance man, heard the crash and came to our aid. He retrieved a ladder and climbed atop the camper. Peter fired up his chain saw, and as I slowly moved backward he "surfed" on the top the camper while simultaneously cutting the tree branch free. Once we were loose he said, "Sorry mate, we've been meaning to cut that tree back."

"Aren't the roads in a camper park meant to have campers on them? I mean, thank you for cutting us loose but how could you let a tree grow like that in the first place?" I asked angrily.

"You are the one who ran into it," he replied.

That point was not in dispute. Nevertheless, it was the wrong thing to say.

"I don't believe this. It's a Goddamn camper park. You didn't keep the road safe, and I think you should pay for at least part of the damages. I want to talk to your boss."

Peter casually called the park owner and left a message. Then he took down my cell phone number and assured me that "one of the blokes who owns this place will call you." I had doubts.

I called the company that rented us the camper. "Technically the awning is on the side of the camper, not the top," I pleaded. "Shouldn't it be covered by our four hundred dollar insurance policy?"

"Sorry, mate," he replied. "If you look at the policy it says the awning on the Leisure Seeker counts as overhead damage." We again considered handing the camper back in, paying the money and being done with it. Instead, we put duct tape over the hole, tied up the awning with a rope, and headed west to the New England Highway.

The New England Highway courses through Australia's Great Dividing Range. One small town follows another and in between are some of Australia's finest national parks. Our route took us though eucalyptus forests and alongside rivers and waterfalls. Not since our safari had we seen such unusual and abundant critters. On one six-mile section of road I saw two kangaroos, an echidna, a wombat, and eight wallabies. Sadly, they were all squished—run over so many times that they had evolved from road kill into "road pizzas."

Our first stop was the sleepy town of Armidale. We arrived late on Friday and were surprised to find that most of the campgrounds were full due to the local dog show. We found a wheelchair for Cami and began to explore. The human participants at the dog show were very friendly, and as soon as they heard our American accent they all asked the same question: "Where are ya from?" followed soon by "How d'ya like Australia?"

These two questions were so predictable that when people would ask where we were from, we would pre-empt the next question by answering, "We are from the U.S. and we think Australia is beautiful. What a great country you have."

Dog shows are an all-day affair. Even though we left before the champion was announced it was already dusk when we found ourselves bumping along a gravel road at twenty miles per hour on our way into Warrambungle National Park. Something big ran up along the passenger side of the camper. Jill let out a scream. It was an emu that didn't like our camper any better than we did. It particularly didn't like our side-view mirror and poked it with a long beak several times before veering off the road and back into the forest.

The huge campground was covered in leaves, and we had it all to ourselves. After dinner, we began roasting "marshies" over a campfire. It was dark and there was no power so we relied on our flashlights to see. "Eye shine" (retinal reflections) were all around us. It was a mob of kangaroos that had become used to people. Tom and Joe put little piles of Cheerios on the ground, and the roos slowly approached to eat them. Tommy held out his hand to one of the animals. A joey—a baby kangaroo—stuck its head out of its mother's pouch and ate out of Tommy's hand.

The quiet was shattered by the collective flapping of wings, and suddenly our peaceful little campground was transformed. Hundreds of screaming sulphur-crested cockatoos made a huge racket—like angry monkeys—but after twenty minutes they flew off as quickly as they had come. They did not stay gone. The racket continued off and on throughout the night. Whenever the cockatoos would arrive screaming, I would wake with a start. When silence resumed I would lie there in my cramped bed next to Tommy and worry about how much it was going to cost to fix the Winnebago. I kept trying to convince myself that "no one was hurt and it's only money." I don't mind spending money, but waste makes me angry. Fixing our rented camper, which we had all grown to hate, was going to be expensive and we would have nothing to show for it except a bill. We were on a budget and an expensive repair would limit our future options.

Worrying wore me down. In the town of Dubbo, our next stop, Joe was teasing Tommy and made him cry. Nothing out of the ordinary—just routine big brother tormenting little brother stuff. By this time in the trip, I was used to Joe acting like an adult, and it took me by surprise when he regressed to behaving like a typical thirteen-year-old. I pulled Joe out the door of the camper and pushed him back against the outside of it. I was getting ready to slap him when Jill yelled for me to stop. Joe ran away and sat on some swings, and I drove to a nearby store where I bought him a protractor and compass—odd make-up gifts, but we were studying geometry. I apologized profusely to the entire family. To Joe's credit, he was very forgiving.

On our way to climb Mount Kosciusko, we went to a platypus reserve. Platypus are shy and rarely show themselves. We waited for over an hour and didn't see any, but we did later see an echidna crossing the road. The echidna looks like a miniature version of a porcupine but with the tubular snout of an anteater. The platypus and the echidna are the world's only monotremes, or egg-laying mammals. Echidnas walk slowly, so slowly that Cami—who was now out of her cast but still limping—was able to catch up to one. When Cami approached, the echidna buried its head and settled into some soft dirt, trying to hide. Cami petted it like she would a dog and was surprised to find that the echidna was not prickly, but soft.

We left the New England Highway and headed for Canberra, Australia's capital. Rounding one corner, we found ourselves staring into the face of an alarmed black and white heifer. She was wedged against a wooden fence and mooing loudly, her eyes wide with fright. A huge brown bull stood behind her, half on top of her. It took a second for me to realize that the two beasts were having what could best be described as vigorous sexual intercourse. As is so often the case in the animal kingdom, this seemed to be his idea more than hers, or so she wanted us to believe.

The boys started giggling. Jill said, "You need to talk with them."

"About what?" I asked.

"About sex."

"They just saw all they needed to know," I replied.

"If you aren't going to talk with them, I will," Jill said. "I think it's pathetic that you are a physician and you still can't have that conversation with your own sons, and by the way that is not all they need to know."

When we arrived in Canberra, we had to drive to four different campgrounds before we found a place to stay. This time, the cause of the crowds was not a dog show. We had unknowingly arrived in Canberra on an historic day—the day of the government apology. During the 1950s, the Australian government took Aboriginal children away from their families and put them in orphanages. This was an attempt to help them fit in to white Australia, and the misguided effort resulted in "the stolen generation" of Aboriginals.

Many countries we visited had carried out evil deeds as part of official government policy, and most never own up to it. On February 13, 2008, we turned on our camper's radio to hear Australia's Prime Minister Kevin Rudd do just that. "The apology," as it is now known, was brief, but humble and moving. The best way to ruin an apology is with an explanation, but Rudd made no attempt to explain or say that "we were only trying to help." He expressed remorse and the hope that this admission would help to heal wounds.

The kids were appalled that the government took children away from their parents, so they didn't complain much when I made them all write essays about the apology. Cami and Tom were in favor of the apology; Joe saw both sides of the issue.

Our next stop was Melbourne, a beautiful city. With great joy, I returned the RV on the outskirts of town and paid the bill for the damages—$2,400. I took the train back downtown to meet the rest of the family, and we went to a Turkish restaurant to celebrate. Tommy walked in and said *"merhaba"* to the man behind the counter, and soon the kids all had a free treat.

The following morning we took the train to the Melbourne Museum. On the first level, the kids each did their museum presentations. Joe talked about a giant squid, Tommy about great white sharks, and Cami about Phar Lap, Australia's greatest racehorse, who was believed to be poisoned with arsenic by American gangsters.

The second level at the museum was devoted to an exhibit called "The Human Body," and it featured life-sized nude photos of people of all ages, from newborn babies to senior citizens. Tommy and Joe were furtively peeking at the pictures of adolescent girls.

A sign advertised a film on the beginning of life and how babies are made.

Jill watched the film alone and decided that the boys should see it. This was a way of having the "sex talk" with visual aids that would not be blocked by our computer's parental filter. Joe said his class had already studied the subject and Tommy simply refused to go. Jill said, "As your teacher, sex education is a required class. I order you to go."

Cami and I were excused. We went to look at the exhibit on blue whales. A whale's enormous skeleton hung from the ceiling of the museum, and we watched a video that showed the museum crew dissecting tons of rancid blubber in hopes of salvaging the skeleton. The stench seemed to ooze through the screen. It was disgusting, but apparently not as awful as the sex education video, judging from the looks on the boys' faces when we met up later. Tommy was pale and shaking his head as though he were the victim of a terrible injustice.

From Melbourne we flew to Hobart, Tasmania, where we were guests of new friends we had met in Gallipoli, Turkey—Tom Watt and Helen Parry and their children Bryn (fourteen), Tom (eleven), and Simon (seven). Tom and Helen are both schoolteachers and had just completed their trip around the world.

After all the time in campgrounds and hotels it was nice to be in the company of friends and to enjoy Helen's incredible home cooking. Tom and Helen knew where to take us and where to avoid. We began with a tour of the Cadbury Chocolate Factory. When the tour ended, we bought "factory seconds" chocolate at a huge discount.

My favorite place was the Frank Hurley Antarctic Museum. Frank Hurley, a native of Sydney, is best known as the photographer on Sir Ernest Shackleton's Imperial Trans-Antarctic Expedition of 1914–1917, when Shackleton and his crew attempted to cross Antarctica. The expedition was a disaster, which made for a great story. Within days of arriving, Shackleton's ship, the *Endurance*, was crushed by the pack ice. Captain and crew took to the lifeboats and went to the closest land they could find—Elephant Island—where they survived on a diet of seal and penguin.

In an attempt to rescue the crew, Shackleton and his sea captain, Frank Worsley, crossed the Southern Ocean in an open-hulled wooden boat only slightly larger than a typical rowboat. Worsley navigated 750 miles using the stars and his sextant to guide them.

When they reached a whaling station on South Georgia Island, Shackleton began planning a rescue operation the next day. Shackleton rescued every man.

I have read many versions of this story and all agree that when circumstances were at their worst, Shackleton was at his best.

"If Shackleton is your hero," Tom said, "why don't we go see his ocean?"

On a beautiful sunny day, Tom, Helen, and their family took us to a "shack" (Australian for "cabin") on Bruny Island, just south of mainland Tasmania, where we made reservations for a boat tour of the Southern Ocean. We arrived at the dock and located Mike, the boat's captain, who was standing in the pilot-house. "What is the weather forecast for today?" I asked. I expected a formal marine weather report on the order of: "A 50 millibar low pressure system has moved in from the Tasman Sea bringing with it a 30 percent chance of precipitation. Winds are westerly and moderate on the Beaufort scale, becoming East/ Southeast. Seas are one to two meters."

Instead, Mike replied, "Weather? No worries, mate."

"Well," I said, "We really want to go. It's just that our whole family is prone to seasickness."

The captain said, "Seasickness? No worries, mate. Take some of these ginger tablets. You'll be right."

Just as Captain Mike predicted, seas were calm and winds were light as we motored out of Adventure Bay, but as we headed south along the east coast of Bruny Island, the weather slowly began to change. The wind increased and the temperature started to fall. When the boat reached Australia's southernmost point, the seas had grown to ten feet and we were no longer able to see over the wave in front of us. Captain Mike pointed south. Above the noise of surf and motor, he called out, "Welcome to the Southern Ocean, mates! Antarctica is that way."

Rain was pouring and the wind began to howl. "Smoke on the water!" Mike hollered. As a child of the 1970s I immediately thought of the song by Deep Purple. I wondered what this had to do with our current predicament. The body of water referred to in that song was Lake Geneva, and we were a long way from there. I looked where Mike was pointing, and sure enough—smoke was billowing off the water.

We later learned that winds of greater than fifty knots are strong enough to lift small droplets off the surface of the water in such abundance that it looks like smoke. An Indian couple on their honeymoon began vomiting what looked like yellow curry off the boat's port side.

This was no ordinary boat ride, nor were we on an ordinary boat. This boat was beautiful, twenty meters long with a rubber pontoon protecting the fiberglass hull and three big outboard engines to power us. We loved it! Captain Mike had certainly made this trip hundreds of times before, but clearly he was excited to be out at sea, and he conveyed a genuine sense of adventure. We missed seeing penguins but we did see albatross on our way back to port, where a complimentary bowl of hot pumpkin soup awaited us.

We were cold and wet, but no one in our family complained. An older British woman ("midging pom" in Australian slang) sure did. "We can't believe you would take us out in weather like that. Were you trying to get us all killed?" she railed. Captain Mike politely replied that yes, the trip had been "a bit dodgy" and no, he had not thought that it would get that rough, but that was all part of the adventure. The woman was having none of his explanation. She stormed off to demand a refund.

Back in port, it was sunny and twenty degrees warmer. The Watts were surprised to hear of the severe weather we encountered. On our way back to the shack, we stopped to fish for squid. "Squiddies" get angry when you bring them out of the water. Bryn learned this the hard way when a squid sprayed ink all over his new shirt. Tom and I walked to a nearby beach to clean the squid, and we did not realize until we were back indoors that our hands were black with ink. Helen cooked the squid with butter and garlic. Tom Watt, Jr., ate his on what may have been the world's first-ever squid, ham, and cheese sandwich.

After a few more lovely days in Tasmania, we headed for New Zealand. In America, we frequently refer to Australia and New Zealand together, much like "bacon and eggs." The countries do have a lot in common, but they are not one and the same, as we soon learned.

CHAPTER 12

NEW ZEALAND

"Doon't Look Doon" and Other Extreme Sports

| *date–date*

Tommy looked forward to Tuesdays. Every Tuesday his "adopted" fourth-grade class in Mesa, Arizona, spent time in the school's computer lab. His classmates visited our website and then e-mailed classroom news and asked Tommy questions about our travels. One student notified us that her parents were participating in the New Zealand Ironman Triathlon during the time we would be in New Zealand, so we decided to volunteer at the event. After landing in Auckland, we rented an old grey minivan and drove to the city of Taupo in the center of New Zealand's North Island.

The next morning we took up our positions at Mile 18 of the final event of the triathlon. The kids handed out orange slices and glasses of Gatorade while Jill and I staffed a three-sided medical tent. By the time the competitors arrived at our station they had already completed a 2.4-mile swim followed by a 112-mile bike race, and they were now 18 miles into the 26-mile run.

We encountered participants with the usual maladies that endurance athletes suffer: muscle cramps, knee pain, and chafed nipples, all worsened by the weather, which was cold, rainy, and windy.

Jill saw a middle-aged woman stagger up to the beverage station and ran out to help her. She guided the woman to the medical tent, moved aside the grill and the white plastic chairs, and cleared a space on the ground. The woman was pale, cold, and had a weak pulse. We eased her down and bundled her in the white cotton blankets provided to us by race officials. Instead of getting better, the woman became confused. Confusion is the hallmark of hypothermia, and endurance athletes' body temperatures plummet once they stop exercising. Furthermore, cotton has no insulating property when wet. It dawned on me that our sodden blankets were making her colder instead of warmer.

Another volunteer dug out an aluminum foil wrapper from the bottom of the first aid kit and with great ceremony unfolded it and lay it atop this lady. "Space Blankets" such as this are supposed to work by trapping radiant body heat but this one didn't help a bit. What this woman needed was wool, a great insulator even when wet. New Zealand has three million people and 60 million sheep—surely someone would have a wool blanket.

We asked the other volunteers and soon the woman was covered with wool blankets. Only then did she improve. (The foil blanket had blown away. Maybe it would be found, cut into pieces, and used to bake potatoes.) After well over an hour, the woman was no longer confused or cold but still vomiting. I dug out one of the anti-nausea tablets from my personal stash and gave it to her, and finally the woman improved enough to go home with her husband.

We had been working in the tent for about four hours when a couple of teenage girls arrived wearing cardinal red "MEDICAL TEAM" shirts identical to ours. Jill and I had been scheduled for the first half of the triathlon, and these were our replacements. The "experienced" girl had taken a first aid class for lifeguards.

The least fit participants had yet to arrive. We told the girls the story of the hypothermic woman and warned them that they may be seeing some sick people. We asked the lifeguard if she had any questions. "Can you get sick if you touch someone else's vomit?" she asked.

"I don't know of any diseases spread by triathlete vomit," I replied. "I think you will be okay."

"See. I told ya," she replied, looking not at me but at her friend.

Worried that these girls were in over their heads, we stayed and helped them out. Jill and I demonstrated how to apply moleskin, how to rub anti-inflammatory cream into cramped muscles, and how to tape an ankle.

The girls were quick studies and what they lacked in formal medical training they made up for with cheerleader enthusiasm, urging people on with shouts of: "Woohoooo! Go finish this race! You got it!" Later, we tried to meet up with the parents of Tommy's classmate, but it never worked out.

New Zealand consists of two islands cleverly named the North Island and the South Island. Together they are about the size of California. As we continued north to visit our friends Shirwin and Judy on the Coromandel Peninsula, the landscape changed to subtropical. We saw silver ferns and even occasional palm trees.

Shirwin and Judy invited us to their home for dinner. They have an elevator and the kids rode it down from the second floor. All three kids got on, but when we met them at the bottom and the elevator doors opened, only Joey and Cami remained. We asked what happened to Tommy. Joe and Cami bobbled their heads and pointed up.

Tommy was spread-eagled some twelve feet above us, his hands and feet wedged across the elevator shaft. He was beginning to lose his grip and pleaded with us to send the elevator back up for him. If he had fallen, I don't think it would have killed him but he quite likely would have joined Cami in "the broken leg club."

As in Australia, we stayed mostly in caravan parks, but this time, instead of renting a camper, we stayed in cabins. This arrangement was ideal for our family. For seventy dollars, we got two bedrooms and a kitchen. At one park in Palmerston North, the owner and his wife asked where we were from.

"America," I replied.

"Oh, good on you," he replied. Then, pointing to his wife he said, "She's a Maori. Do you know about them?"

"Not much," I answered.

"Cannibals," he replied. "Her grandfather was one a dem that ate Captain Cook's men. No worries though—she's had a proper dinner tonight and besides she doesn't like the way Americans taste so she probably won't eat your family," he said with a smile. His wife rolled her eyes and shook her head. Clearly she had heard it all before.

Maori are believed to be of Polynesian descent. They arrived in New Zealand about eight hundred years ago. This makes New Zealand one of the newest countries on the planet in terms of human habitation. By contrast, aboriginals are thought to have lived in Australia for thirty thousand years.

British soldiers fought the Maori for control of New Zealand, and the Maori frequently won. When the Maori chief Rewi Maniapoto said, "We will fight on forever, forever, forever," he meant it. The British wisely decided to make peace with the Maori at the Treaty of Waitangi. Whether this treaty was duplicitous remains a topic of debate.

Invaders and indigenous people typically don't get along well, but in New Zealand today, Maori and white New Zealanders seem to have a good relationship. The New Zealand National Rugby Team, known as "The All Blacks," is composed of both Maori and white New Zealanders. They begin each rugby match with a traditional Maori dance known as a "haka," which is the equivalent of the New York Yankees starting each baseball game with a Cherokee rain dance.

As we made our way to the South Island, we spent our days enjoying extreme sports: ropes courses, monster truck driving, sky swings, and zorbing. We took a gondola up the side of Mount Ngongotaha and then coasted down the curvy mountain road in an unpowered go-kart-like vehicle. Of all the extreme sports activities available, this one was the tamest, so on our second trip down I decided to spice things up. As Tommy and I raced down the road I bumped him and he vanished off the road.

"No big deal," I thought. "The fence will stop him." After the next two hairpin turns, I looked up and saw that there was no fence, only a cliff over which Tommy had fallen. He had dropped thirty feet down the mountainside and the only thing that kept him from going further was the metal signpost that Tommy was now straddling. The sign read: "Slow down." Tommy was crying. He had a big bruise on the middle of his right thigh. He wanted to stop, but I promised not to run into him again and he slowly continued to the bottom.

The capital of extreme sports is the South Island city of Queenstown. It was here that Joe made known his desire to bungee jump. Tommy, whose leg was now better, said he also wanted to try it. I remained noncommittal, thinking I would make a last-minute decision based on safety.

As we approached the sales counter, Tommy was petrified. He gingerly stepped on the scale. He weighed 76 pounds—one pound too light to take the plunge. I watched as a look of relief briefly flashed across his face, but then he began acting disappointed. He had to. He had no choice, because his big brother was standing right there. "Oh, man. I can't believe that. I'm only one pound away," he said. "That sucks. I wanted to go so bad." The office sold bottled water, and all Tommy would have to do was drink a liter, and he would have been fine, but I didn't say anything.

It was my turn to get on the scale.

"Triple digit club, mate."

"What?" I asked.

"101 kilos [225 pounds]. We don't see too many of those," said the operator as he drew the number "101" with a big black marker on the back of my left hand.

"Does that mean I'm too fat to go?"

"No, you can go," he said, leaving unanswered my question about whether I was too fat.

"Have you ever had any fatalities?" I asked.

"None today," he replied.

"I mean it," I said. "Have there been any deaths or serious injuries such as broken necks?"

"No. Not one," he answered.

I asked how many people have jumped, and the answer was reassuring: "Approximately fifteen thousand per year for twenty years."

As a man of science, I was greatly comforted by these statistics—right up until I walked onto the Kawarau Bridge.

A second staff member had tied my feet together and clipped on the bungee cord. I stood on the bridge, staring down at the river 141 feet below. I remembered Mr. Hanick's high school physics class, and I thought about what would happen to me when the bungee cord broke—which I knew it would. To free fall is to feel weightless the same way astronauts do in space, but in actuality by accelerating downward at 9.8 meters per second squared, I would be gaining a tremendous amount of kinetic energy. By the time I hit the water, I would be traveling at 29 meters per second, or 65 miles per hour.

As I suddenly decelerated to zero, the water would feel the same as concrete. The attachments that held my body together would suffer mechanical failure. My liver would tear loose from the back of my abdomen. The dura mater would become untethered from my skull, causing part of my brain to explode out my ears and nose. My heart would be bruised so badly that it would stop. There would be horrible pain, but only for a moment. The impact would tenderize the rest of me, so my 101 kg would be more easily digested by the salmon in the river below.

My mind then raced forward to my closed casket funeral. I pitied the poor bastard who would have to give the eulogy. What would he say? "It was how he would have wanted to go." Or maybe, "It beats dying in a nursing home." No matter how well he chose his words or how seamlessly he delivered them, every man, woman, and child in that church would be shaking their heads and thinking the exact same thing about me: "What an imbecile!"

"Doon't look doon." The call from the bungee operator brought me back to reality.

"What?" I had become accustomed to New Zealand accents, but this accent was Scottish, and the man seemed to be slurring his words. "What did you say?" I asked.

Pointing at the river, he yelled, "Doon't look doon! Jump oot, away from the platform."

"Oot?"

"Yes. Oot. If you doon't, you might hit yer head."

My legs were bound together with a towel, but they were so wet with sweat I was afraid I was going to slip right out. The black "101" mark of shame on my pale left hand was starting to run. I was dizzy.

The drunk Scotchman said, "Wave to yer friends und family—yer on camera, ya know."

I waved goodbye to the soon-to-be widow and orphans. Then I yelled, "I changed my mind! I don't want to go! I don't know why I signed up. I am terrified of heights. I don't want to go."

"Acchh—just joomp. I'll coont backwards from five and when I get to zero, go."

"I don't care if you coont from a million, I'm not going," I said.

"It's non-refoondable."

"What?"

"You heard me," he said.

"Not even half?" This guy knew the perfect button to push.

"Zero."

"Have there ever been any fatalities?"

"None today." (They must have taught all the staff to say that.) "Just joomp."

For reasons that remain a mystery to me, when the man finished counting backwards, I did what I was told. I jumped.

At no time did I believe that the bungee cords might actually work until I felt the slightest tug on my legs. After I stopped bouncing, I came to rest suspended by my feet above the river until two men paddled out in a raft and lowered me down. "How was it?" one of the men asked.

I felt the back of my pants. "Well, I didn't shit myself."

"I'm happier about that than you are, mate."

Joe experienced none of my terror and enjoyed his jump.

I'm sure New Zealand must have some problem areas, but we didn't see them. It was twenty-three days of fun in a country with welcoming locals and spectacular and diverse scenery. There were not many animals though; in fact, New Zealand only has one native mammal: a bat. All the other mammals—mostly possums—are non-native species that we were encouraged to run over because they have decimated native bird populations.

In Christchurch, over dinner at Hell Pizza, we realized that the time to leave this wonderful county was at hand and we had not learned much about it.

We spent our last three days trying to do so. I read the kids a book about New Zealand history, we saw a kiwi bird and a 110-year-old tuatara lizard. We attended a Maori cultural show, where we saw a haka dance performed. This aggressive dance features huge tattooed Maori men who scream, grunt, slap their thighs, stick out their tongues, and finish with a "slit your throat" gesture.

What a perfect dance to frighten away Captain Cook or prepare for an aggressive sport like rugby.

CHAPTER 13

ARGENTINA

Food Good; Salsa Man Bad | *March 23–April 21, 2008*

*T*he twelve-hour flight from Auckland, New Zealand, to Buenos Aires, Argentina, was the longest of the trip. We left Auckland at 5 p.m. on Easter Sunday, crossed the International Dateline, and arrived in Buenos Aires at 1 p.m.—still on Easter Sunday. The International Dateline and the resurrection of our Lord have always been big mysteries to me, and experiencing both on the same day, along with jet lag, was exhausting and confusing. The kids felt the same way. Even two helpings of Easter candy and two additional dollar snacks were not enough to perk them up.

In the year 2000, we couldn't have afforded to visit Argentina, which was then one of the most expensive countries on earth. In 2001, Argentina messed its pants, financially speaking. Inflation was rampant, unemployment was high. At that time, the Argentine peso was fixed to the U.S. dollar at an exchange rate of 1:1. People could deposit and withdraw their money in either pesos or dollars and get the same number of either.

As financial conditions became desperate, people began to withdraw their money from the banks. Unions staged a nationwide strike, and middle-class people took to the streets of Buenos Aires, banging pots and pans in what became known as the *cacerolazo* (from the Spanish word for pan). Officials then closed the banks altogether and allowed the peso to "float." A better term would have been "sink," because when all was said and done the Argentine peso was worth one U.S. quarter.

When the banks finally reopened, withdrawals were permitted only in the now-devalued pesos. Early the next year, the government defaulted on $140 billion of international debt, the biggest default in history. A lot of wealth went to money heaven (or money hell, if you believe in such things), and for travelers Argentina transformed overnight from being an expensive country to a travel value.

We needed to get from the airport to the hotel in Buenos Aires, but as we feared the taxi driver didn't take any credit cards and our ATM card didn't work. Jill got in line to trade in our US $200 in New Zealand currency for Argentine pesos. The clerk looked askance at the New Zealand money, as though Jill had printed it herself. We patiently explained that, unlike Argentina, New Zealand had never defaulted on its debt and was in great shape economically. This English macro-economics lesson was wasted on the Spanish-speaking clerk. She shook her head and waved us out of the way.

We convinced the taxi driver to take us without paying. He let us know this was highly unusual and that he expected a big tip for taking a chance. When we got to the hotel, we convinced the clerk to loan us forty dollars with our credit card as collateral until I could re-activate our ATM card. Both of these transactions were made easier by the fact that we were traveling as a family, which apparently made us seem more trustworthy.

About 5 p.m. we decided to have an early second Easter dinner and then go to bed. We walked up the street to a restaurant, but the sign out front said they did not open until 9 p.m. We walked along avenue 9 de Julio, which was nine lanes wide and packed with traffic. We found an old-fashioned playground with swings and a teeter totter where we hung out for a while. Then we made our way back to the restaurant, where we waited until 9.

Cami wanted a steak. One was listed on the menu for the equivalent of six dollars, so we ordered it, expecting a hamburger. She was served a filet mignon and a huge pile of mashed potatoes that were absolutely delicious! This was our first introduction to the wonders of Argentine food. We all were falling asleep at the dinner table but managed to make it back to the hotel, proud that we had the discipline to stay awake until 11 p.m. We thought this would help us adjust to the new time zone, but at 3 a.m. we all were wide awake. So were our next-door neighbors.

We had knocked on many doors on this trip, asking our neighbors to stop yelling or to turn down loud music, but these people were conversing at normal volume, and asking them to not speak didn't seem right. We turned on the television and watched a soccer match (one is always on in Argentina, regardless of time of day) but even that didn't help us fall asleep. Reluctantly, I passed out sleeping pills. That worked for the kids, but thirty minutes later I was still wide awake. I took another pill and washed it down with some delicious three dollar Argentine Cabernet.

We rolled out of bed the following day at 2 p.m. and wandered bleary-eyed around Buenos Aires. We all fell asleep about midnight, but once again we woke up at 3 a.m., and once again we needed medication to get back to sleep. This time

I tried for a placebo effect with the kids. I gave them ibuprofen and told them it was "super strong sleepy medicine" and that Winkin', Blinkin' and Nod were going to visit them very soon. Tommy asked why I was talking baby talk.

This was the first time I had ever given someone a placebo. It didn't work. I gave the kids the real stuff about an hour later. I was beginning to feel like Elvis's doctor. We continued to sleep until 2 p.m. every day. When we were awake, we all were in a fog.

Jill and I did go out one evening to a tango show. Before we left, I gave Joe the passports along with strict instructions about what to do if we didn't come back. We let the front desk clerk know where we were going. We had a cell phone with us, along with the number of the hotel. We took the bus across town to the show. After the show, it was raining so we decided to take a cab to the hotel instead of the bus. On the way we saw riot police and protesters banging their pans in the rain. The protest was expected to be a big one, in reaction to the government's decision to tax beef exports, but the rain had had a calming effect.

After four days, the family finally slept through the night without drugs. It was a good thing, too, because the next morning we were up at 5 a.m. to catch a plane to San Carlos de Bariloche, a city of seventy-seven thousand in the foothills of the Andes. We arrived on a Friday, right between summer high season and winter ski season. Our first day in town, we walked by a lovely little *panaderia* (bakery), where we bought cookies and cakes. The bill for the whole family was four dollars.

Because we were spending two months in South America, we wanted to learn Spanish. We arranged a Spanish immersion program that included a home stay and two weeks of Spanish school. The school would teach us grammar, the home stay Argentine culture. We booked the home stay through the language school well ahead of time and paid for it up front. (Apart from our safari, that was the only time we did that the entire year.) Here is the description we received from the school:

The only family which could accommodate you in Bariloche is not really a family. It is a lady of about 60 who lives alone. She has a son who visits her very often. She has cats and dogs and lives in a very big house; it has 6 bedrooms and 4 bathrooms, a living room and dining room. She will prepare breakfast and dinner for you; lunch will be on your own.

As our home stay didn't begin until Sunday, we spent the first two nights in a hotel. We were looking forward to being welcomed into a family's home. Cami couldn't wait to meet the cats and dogs. I was excited that we would finally have a quiet night in Argentina. To get off on the right foot, we bought our hosts a big cake with chocolate frosting. We left our luggage at our hotel and walked more than a mile, first up steps and then up a hillside.

When we arrived at the house, I expected to be sniffed by a cat or a dog, but there were no pets. There was a man named Don Julio. He was a tall, heavyset bald man in his sixties, a dentist by trade with an office downstairs. His wife, Anna, was an accountant. They had two grown children, both of whom had moved away. The house had a large common room with two separate wings. We needed a ride back to get our luggage, but the couple didn't offer, so I used my cell phone to call a cab.

School began at eight on Monday morning, and we were nervous. School meant structured days, and we all had grown accustomed to a free, unstructured way of life. We were given a pre-test and then separated based on our ability. Jill and I were in the second level adults. All three kids were in children's beginners. Here is Joe's journal entry:

We wake up at 7:00 and walk 10 blocks in the biting wind and come to the cheery warmth of the school. We usually play games (i.e. hangman, scrabble, opposites) then have our first break. After that I do Spanish exercise while Cami and Tommy fight over massa (the Spanish word for play dough). After the second break we do vocabulary and play some more Spanish games and Evon (our teacher) writes up our homework.

Argentine food was by far the best of the trip, and the Italian food in Argentina was superb. When Anna said we would be having spaghetti our first night, Tommy couldn't wait because spaghetti is his favorite food. Sadly, Anna's sauce tasted like ketchup. The next morning, the "breakfast" that awaited was of a loaf of bread sitting next to a half-full pot of cold, stale coffee. The cake we brought on Sunday had not been served to us at dinner but we saw a large piece of it wrapped and sitting high on a shelf—clearly not meant for us.

We learned that Don Julio's salsa band had practice on Tuesdays and Thursdays in the dental office on the floor below the wing of the house in which we were staying. The music would begin at 10 p.m. and would go until 1 in the morning. Here is Joe's journal entry:

The Salsa house is our home stay for 2 weeks. It was OK for the first 2 nights but on Tuesday we discovered that our host played in a salsa band. His band arrived at 10PM and played and drank wine until 1 AM. This would happen every Tuesday and Thursday. Jet lag was bad when we first arrived in Buenos Aires, but "salsa lag" is worse because I have to go to school at 7am every morning.

Jill asked Evon, one of our school teachers, about the lack of hospitality at our home stay. Is this how Argentines typically treat guests? Or was it just that Don Julio was an ass-holio? Evon said that staying up late was an Argentine tradition—part of the culture, as it were. At least Anna was an incredible cook, *si*? And her husband, the teachers said, was an expert fisherman. The boys and I like to fish, so I asked Don Julio if he could recommend someone to take us out. He replied, "I am a busy man who is dedicated to my music. I have no time for fishing."

Jill went to a drugstore and bought earplugs for everyone. It helped a little, but we could still hear the bass as they played the same song over and over. Despite all their practice, the band was not very good. I was torn between not wanting to make a scene and sticking up for my family. On the one hand, staying up late was part of Argentine culture, we were guests in their home, we were representatives of our country and didn't want to be seen as ugly Americans. On the other hand, we were paying them, and playing loud music when children are trying to sleep is inconsiderate, no matter what your culture.

Based on Evon's advice, I kept silent. I stayed awake watching TV and when Don Julio finally came upstairs at 2 a.m., I gave him my best icy stare. Salsa practice continued. These were awkward days, and as time passed we skipped Anna's dinners and ate out.

The town itself was charming. Here is what Joe had to say:

Bariloche is beautiful. It is surrounded by mountains and built on the shores of Lake Nahuel Huai. Sometimes we would ice skate in a rink literally jutting out over the lake.

When our morning school session has ended, we usually go eat lunch at one of Bariloche's fantastic restaurants. Then we get our dollar snacks at Mamuscka. Mamuscka is a chocolate marvel.

Argentina was making us fat. My 101 kg in New Zealand had swelled to 105 and would have been worse but I continued to run four times per week. I only had one pair of running shorts so after running I would wash them out in the shower and then hang them over a heater to dry. I did this in Salsa Man's house, and when I emerged from the shower, my shorts were in flames. I quickly put out the fire, but big holes had been burned in the seat.

Later that week, we visited an *estancia* (farm) owned by a German who immigrated to Argentina. We went horseback riding on the pampas—an enormous grassland that covers a large part of Argentina. On a windy day, we mounted lovely, well-tended horses and headed out for a ride. Our guide was a genuine gaucho named Ignacio.

Riding along, we thought we saw tumbleweeds in the distance, but on closer inspection they were fleet-footed, dirt-colored birds. These were South American *nandu*, the same birds Eddie had told us about seven months previously in Tanzania. Midway through the ride, it began to pour rain. We headed for shelter at one of the farmhouses, where a traditional lunch of *asado* (grilled meat) and red wine awaited us.

Our two weeks at the home stay were coming to an end, but rather than stay Friday and Saturday night in Casa de Anna, we called a cab and asked the driver to take us to a cheap hotel on Bariloche's main street.

Our Spanish was improving, and by the end of two weeks it was passable enough that we didn't need to fall back on English to be understood. Our next stop was the tiny village of El Chaltén, some eight hundred miles to the south. We were on the last bus out of town for the season, as few people go that far south during the winter. Even the penguins head for warmer climates. The bus ride started out along paved mountainous roads but soon gave way to *ruta cuaranta* (route 40), a dirt road that passed through the pampas. Here is Cami's description:

April 13, 2008:

Today we went on a bus trip. It lasted 2 days. On the bus trip we saw a loma hop a fence and we saw some nandu. The are big and fast and brown and look like an ostrich. Our driver caught a armadillo. I got to tuch the armadillo. He was so cute. The hole bus trip was on a dirt road, but the bus trip wasn't as bad as I thought it would be. There were lots of nice people on the bus. It was very pretty outside.

After twelve hours on the bus, we stopped at a *vagabundo* motel in the tiny town of Perito Moreno. We paid twenty-four dollars for two dirty rooms with cold showers and light bulbs that hung from the ceiling on bare wires. On the lobby wall was a plaque stating that Butch Cassidy and the Sundance Kid hid out nearby.

Our bald-tired bus was late the next morning, and I went to buy some dollar snacks at the local grocery store. There was nothing to buy. The farmers' strike whose protests we had witnessed in Buenos Aires had caused food shortages in Argentina's rural south. Still, every petrol station in Argentina has a large pot of boiling water out front for *yerba maté*, the traditional Argentine tea made from dried leaves and twigs.

We still had ten more hours to go on the twenty-six-hour bus trip. One of our fellow passengers approached Jill and said, "When I saw your kids get on this bus, I thought 'Oh no, this is going to be a nightmare, I'll be listening to them whine for two whole days,' but they are incredibly well behaved and man-nerly. You and your husband have done a great job." Jill and I were flattered by his comments, but at this point in the trip, we had come to expect good behavior. Joey, Tommy, and Cami were now experienced travelers who tolerated long trips without complaining, even though most of their electronic distractions (iPods and PSPs) were now broken.

We finally arrived at our destination: the town of El Chaltén (population 371), which was built in 1985 to help secure a border dispute with Chile. A wide spot in the Rio de Las Vueltas valley, El Chaltén consists of two tiny stores, a campground, a youth hostel, and an out-of-order ATM.

One frosty morning at 6 a.m., I walked out of our youth hostel and within minutes passed a sign that read "Los Glacieres National Park." I was alone on the trail and after walking a mile uphill surrounded by trees in golden fall color, I got my first view of Cerro Fitzroy (10,262 feet) with its rugged granite peaks and its great glacier pouring out in front—a vision I will never forget.

Cerro Fitzroy is also called Cerro Chaltén, which means "smoking moun-tain" in Tehuelche because a cloud usually forms around the mountain. I took a few pictures and then put the camera back in my pocket, knowing that a more wide-open view lay ahead, but in the ten minutes it took me to arrive there, clouds had formed, blanketing the mountain peak. I hiked another four miles all the way to the glacier but I never saw Cerro Fitzroy again.

From El Chaltén we took the bus to El Calafate, home to the Perito Moreno Glacier. Most glaciers in the world are retreating, but Perito Moreno is advancing. We didn't have a place to stay in El Calafate, and we ended up at the apartment of a woman who was waiting when the bus arrived. After we unpacked, we heard scratching at the door. The tan puppy's name was Luna, and Cami soon had her tucked under a blanket.

That night we went to an all-you-can-eat buffet restaurant. I have no idea why. We never finished a meal the entire time we were in Argentina, so every restaurant was essentially "all you can eat." Kids age five and under ate for four dollars; adult meals cost ten dollars. To Jill's great embarrassment, I told Tommy (now age ten) to say he was *cinco* and Cami was *cuatro*.

We asked the waitress if she could put the bones left from our four-dollar steaks into a bag to bring home to Luna. She returned to the table carrying a plastic bag filled with steak and sausage. We explained that we only wanted a few bones, but it was no use. As we carried the grocery bag back to our cabana, stray dogs followed us the entire way. That night, in addition to the usual Argentine banter until 3 a.m., we had dogs whining at our door. Cami stayed awake most of the night, feeding them sausage.

We had mixed emotions when it was time to leave Argentina. We loved what Argentina had to offer us—especially the spectacular scenery and incredible food—but unlike most other destinations, we never felt welcomed. We departed El Calafate and traveled via bus across the Andes to Chile.

CHAPTER 14

CHILE

A Simple Day Hike | *April 22–May 14, 2008*

*C*hile charges every U.S. citizen one hundred dollars to fly into the country, but it is free to enter by land or by sea, so we saved five hundred dollars and took a bus to the border crossing high atop the Patagonian Andes.

Patagonia is a geographic region in southern South America, part Argentina, and part Chile. Magellan named this area "Patagon," which means "land of the giants" because the average height of the Tehuelche natives was 5 feet, 11 inches. The average Spaniard of that day measured just 5 feet, 1 inch.

Our first stop in Chile was Puerto Natales, the southernmost point on our trip. Our bus arrived just as school had been dismissed for the day and we wheeled our luggage amid uniformed school kids until we found an inexpensive little hotel. At eight the next morning, we woke up refreshed after our first undisturbed night in over a month—a night with no salsa music and no 3 a.m. conversations to wake us.

From Puerto Natales, we hired a van and driver and traveled three hours south on a gravel road to Torres del Paine National Park. Fall is the windiest time of year in Patagonia. Shortly after arriving in the park we got out to take some photos of a glacier. Joe was able to lean into the wind and have it hold him at a 45-degree angle to the road. I was sitting up front next to the driver, and when we returned to the van I noticed a new crack in the windshield. A piece of gravel, propelled by the wind, had blown up off the road and cracked the windshield while the van was parked.

After three days in Puerto Natales, we were ready to move north. Our options were a bus, a plane, or a cattle freighter. Flying would have been wonderful, as the journey would have taken us over the southern Patagonian ice fields. Next to Antarctica and Greenland, the southern Patagonian ice fields are the largest in the world. But that flight was far too expensive. The bus was cheaper but the only road north would have taken us back the way we had just come through Argentina. Our third option was a cattle freighter.

Due to concerns about hoof and mouth disease (Argentina has it, Chile doesn't), Chilean cattle cannot come back into Chile after passing through Argentina. So the cattle all go by freighter through the remote Chilean fiords. The freighter company added cabins to accommodate truck drivers and a few tourists. It was a fraction of the cost of flying and took about the same time as the bus.

Our biggest concern was rough seas. I walked to the dock in Puerto Natales and talked to the freighter's booking agent. He said, "No problem. No one gets sick. You will be fine." I had heard this before. Looking over his shoulder and out his office window, I could see whitecaps on the bay.

"Are you sure?" I asked.

"Si. Por supeuesto." ("Yes. Of course.") He seemed offended that I believed my own eyes instead of him.

Our ship, the M/V Puerto Eden, was scheduled to depart on Friday, but due to weather it couldn't dock until Saturday. The same agent who sold us the tickets helped us board the ship. He said to us, "Cuidado. El oceano es muy malo."

"What did he say?" Cami asked.

"He said to be careful, that the ocean is very sick," Tommy replied.

We walked past the trailers packed with mooing cattle to a freight elevator that led to the cabin deck. The rest of the family was in the four-berth A-class suites, while I bunked with the truck drivers on the same deck as the cows.

The next morning, it seemed the booking agent had been telling the truth. The sea was so calm that the only way to sense movement was to look at the rugged shoreline. Sailors covet calm water. The labyrinthine route through the Chilean fiords was testament to the extremes they would go to get it. The Puerto Eden repeatedly turned left and then right, moving past shipwrecks in the narrow channels.

The water was calm, but the weather was cold. We were allowed on the inside bridge of the vessel with Captain Rodrigo and his crew. Even though the ship was equipped with a GPS and Loran, most of the navigation through the fiords was done the old-fashioned way, with binoculars, a chart, and a compass. Captain Rodrigo spoke excellent English. He pointed to Joe and Cami and said, "These two children are yours, right?" I nodded yes. He then pointed to Tommy and said, "How do you know the Chileno?"

I replied, "He is mine too. What makes you think he is Chilean?"

"He talks just like a Chilean," said the captain. "His pronunciation is perfect."

On the third day, we left the calm waters of the fiords and entered the Chilean Sea. The waves climbed to eight feet. Joe tolerated these high seas well, but the rest of us were motion sick. This time ginger tablets and Dramamine were not enough so we took to our bunks and waited for calmer water.

In keeping with our tradition of miserable holidays, this was Cami's eighth birthday. The crew baked a cake for the occasion, but we waited to serve it until the seas calmed the following day.

Cami worried about the cows. They had now been packed together, unable to move in their trailers, for three days. We no longer heard them, but we did smell them as three days of urine and stool lent a feculent odor to the ship. "Why don't they take them out for a walk?" Cami asked.

The next morning we arrived in the Chilean town of Puerto Montt where we rented a car, drove onto a ferry, and traveled to the town of Ancud on Chiloé Island. Chiloé is Chile's second-largest island and is culturally different from the rest of Chile. The people of Chiloé still believe in witches and trolls, the most famous of which is the *trauco*. According to legend, the trauco is a troll that inhabits the woods of Chiloé. Despite his ugly appearance, the trauco has a seductive magnetism that attracts young women. If a single woman becomes pregnant and no one steps forward as the father, people assume the trauco to be the missing parent. This excuses the woman from fault, because the trauco is irresistible.

Ancud is a small, poor fishing village on Chiloé. At night Ancud fills with smoke from the wood fires that are used for both heating and cooking. When we checked into a hostel overlooking the sea, we asked the owner if there were any penguins nearby. He said he thought the penguins had all gone "home." If there were any left in the area, he said they would be at Puñihuil.

The following morning we set out for the Islotes Puñihuil National Monument, an hour's drive over dirt roads. We saw beautiful ocean vistas—and no homes—for miles. We were driving down the road, penguins on our minds, when a man jumped in front of the car and began waving his arms. I braked hard.

"*Hola*," he shouted.

"*Hola*," I responded. "*Que pasa?*"

"*Vengan conmigo a mi barco.*"

Joey asked, "What did he say?"

I replied, "He wants us to go with him to his boat."

Tommy said, "I think he is drunk."

Cami commented, "I think he is just happy."

I asked, "*El pinguino esta aquí?*" (Are there any penguins here?)

Our new friend replied, "*Si, pero solo dos.*" (Yes, but only two.)

For ten dollars he took us all for a penguin safari in his rasta-colored skiff. We came upon two sea otters. They have a reputation for playfulness, but these two wouldn't leave each other alone. The bigger sea otter kept lying on top the smaller one and trying to push it under water. The smaller sea otter kept trying to bite the bigger one. Our captain laughed. It dawned on me that maybe they were doing more than just playing. "Hey Jill, I think they are . . ."

Jill replied, "I know what they are doing."

We hadn't been alone much during the past year, and I hoped that watching frisky sea otters might put her in the mood. "Honey, when we get back to the hotel, do you want to pretend we are sea otters?" I asked. Jill answered *sotto voce*.

We saw cormorants and sea lions, but no penguins. We dragged the skiff back onto the beach, and our captain suggested we go have some lunch at a restaurant on the beach nearby. With a little luck, maybe a penguin would turn up. "Loco empanadas" were the specialty. "Loco" turned out to be a delicious local species of abalone. Lunch cost four dollars for the entire family, and when we left the restaurant Tommy yelled "penguin!" and pointed to the middle of the beach where stood a solitary Humboldt penguin. "He stay here," said our boat captain "He has no family." The captain fed the penguin a herring, and the penguin waddled back into a stinky metal shed.

"Well, we saw ourselves a penguin, the last of the flightless birds," Joe said.

I responded, "He keeps him in a shed. That's not in the wild."

"He has no family. We saw him on the beach," said Jill. "That counts as the wild."

Two days later we drove from our nice hotel in Ancud to Cucao, a tiny hamlet with nothing to offer except its proximity to Chiloé Islands National Park. We looked for somewhere to stay, but found nothing—no hotels, campgrounds, or even a store. After searching for more than two hours, we finally found a woman who had a home where we could stay. Casa de Luz was filthy, and freezing cold. The owner was not all that pleasant, either. None of us got any rest, and the next morning Luz complained, while smoking a cigarette, that the aroma of the eggs we were cooking was going to make her laundry smell funny.

We went for a drive along a deserted beach. In the distance we noticed a man dressed in overalls fishing in the surf using green monofilament line wrapped around a tin can with a stick through a hole in the middle of the can. We stood nearby and watched him reel in four fish. Then we began to communicate with him using a combination of pantomime and broken Spanish. The fisherman had two large burlap bags, one filled with the fish he had caught and the other filled with brown, squishy sea cucumbers. He was using these for bait, as well as snacks.

He demonstrated how to tear them open. With a dirty finger he scooped out some of the squishy insides and insisted they tasted "*muy bien.*"

Tommy sensed an opportunity to win the one hundred-dollar family prize for eating the most disgusting thing on the trip. So far, we had eaten Argentine blood sausage, seared kangaroo, and crocodile; compared with those, raw sea cucumber was a sure winner. He reached into the fisherman's bag and pulled out a big one. Tommy stuck his fingers inside and scooped out the sea cucumber innards, which were pink with streaks of yellow and, according to Tommy, tasted very salty.

Joe cannot stand to be beaten by his brother. He grabbed a hunk of sea cucumber, held it in his fingers, and then with great drama dropped it into his open mouth. His plan was to drop it straight to the back of his throat and into his esophagus (the way a mom feeds a baby bird) without having to taste it, but he gagged and the phlegm-textured sea cucumber came back up atop his tongue. Joe made a face and swallowed hard.

Neither boy asked for seconds.

After a pleasant hike along the beach, we began driving back to Ancud. You see a lot of stray dogs in Chile, and as we rounded a corner, I noticed what appeared to be a fat, orange-colored dog with a face like a wombat. When it loped away, we realized it wasn't a dog after all. The animal was a pudu deer. These small deer are endangered, shy, and rarely seen during daytime.

The pudu must have been a herald of Mother Earth's restlessness, because when we crested the next hill we saw a huge plume of smoke that was grey on the bottom and white on the top, rising far above the clouds. We asked some road crew workers what was going on, and they explained that this was Chile's largest volcanic eruption in seventy years.

As we stood by the roadside and stared silently at the volcano, it occurred to me that our miserable previous night in Cucao had led to the amazing events of this day. If not for the night at Casa De Luz, we never would have met the fisherman, seen the pudu, or witnessed the erupting volcano. The whole day was predicated on our willingness to move from the comfort of Ancud to the unknowns of Cucao. It was no different than deciding whether or not to look for fossils in Utah, only this time adventure trumped practicality and I was glad it did.

I felt obliged to point out to the kids that we were in the footsteps of Charles Darwin. He had docked in Puerto Natales in the 1835 and had been seasick almost daily on the *Beagle*. Darwin had complained about the smoke in Ancud, and while visiting Cucao, he witnessed an eruption of the Osorno volcano (the natives are said to have blamed this on a witch).

We planned a kayaking trip to a remote part of Chiloé the following morning but our guide canceled due to high winds. This was fine with Joe and Tom, both of whom had a mysterious case of diarrhea. The volcano was now visible only on CNN, where reports made it seem as if half of South America had been blown off into space. A more realistic report came from a friend of ours in Puerto Natales, who has a friend in Chaiten. Here is the firsthand account:

As you may know one of the local volcanoes went into eruption. The evacuation went well. The town is small and people help each other here. People were calm. The local radio was an enormous help in communicating and luckily it was Saturday. There is no running water, for the local water supply is contaminated by the ash. Also the livestock and cattle are not able to find fresh forage.

We read this to the kids and asked how they felt. Joey said, "On the one hand it was cool to see a volcano erupting, but I feel bad for the people who had to leave their homes. And I hope those weren't the same cows that we saw on the freighter—that would be horrible luck."

After witnessing an erupting volcano, we moved north to try to climb one. Chile is home to 40 percent of the world's active volcanoes. The volcanoes run south to north along the Andes and make up the southeastern part of the famous Ring of Fire that stretches as far north as the Aleutian Islands and as far west as the Philippines.

The beautiful town of Pucón is dominated by the snow-covered, perfectly cone-shaped Villarrica Volcano, which boasts an altitude of 2,800 meters (9,240 feet). During the day, smoke can be seen rising from the volcano. At night, an eerie red glow emanates from the top. Joe and Tommy were excited that they were going to get to see molten lava in the cauldron of an active volcano.

The local fire department has a model of a stop light out front that represents the risk of eruption. Green is low, yellow is moderate, red means "evacuate the town." The last minor eruption took place in 1984, when a small amount of lava trickled down the mountain. The last major eruption was in 1971.

The boys and I have been backpacking together for years, and before we set out they would typically ask how difficult the hike was going to be. For the Villarrica Volcano, they didn't bother. This was just a *day hike* after all. How hard can a *day hike* be? Besides, the light outside the fire station was green and green means go. Sure it was a 1,400-meter (4,500 feet) ascent in only 4 kilometers (2.4 miles), but people do it all the time. Maybe I should have wondered when we went to the climbing store the day before to talk with our guides and get fitted for crampons. Maybe I should have wondered when the guides said the hike would take nine hours. Maybe I should have wondered just by walking outside and looking at the damn volcano.

Joe, Tommy, and I arrived at the base of the peak at 8 a.m. along with our two guides, Rodrigo and Sebastian. The other climbers all appeared fit and in their twenties. No other kids were there, and I was the only person with grey hair. Thanks to Argentine food and my incinerated running shorts, I was heavier than ever.

Many hikes start gradually, but this was tough right from the start. Here is what Tommy wrote:

It was the hardest thing I've ever done. The first part was about a mile all uphill. Then we got to a glacier which was really fun to climb on. I don't really know why but it just was. The next part was the hardest it was almost vertical skree with cliffs on either side of us.

After three hours of hiking many of the fit-looking twenty-somethings had turned around, but we carried on. Several climbers asked Tommy his age and seemed impressed when he answered, *"Diez."* Tommy never complained. He was roped to Rodrigo in case of a fall. Joe and I were not wearing harnesses.

It was hard to tell how competent our guides were. They would tell us when to rest, but apart from that they were silent. In poorer countries such as Chile, just because a guide will take you does not mean they should take you. They sometimes care more about your money than your safety.

We were the last to reach the summit that day, and we didn't linger for long. The lava we were hoping to see was covered with a layer of smoke that stunk like rotten eggs. Tommy gagged at the smell and then had a hard fall and bruised his knee.

The majority of serious mountaineering injuries are due to falls that occur on descent, and as we started down, we soon found ourselves on sharp, steep, loose talus. Here is Joe's description:

Picture a sharp pile of rocks not connected to the ground in any way at a 100 degree angle while carrying a pack and you get the hardest moment of this entire trip.

We were in a tight spot. The kids were exhausted. The wind was blowing, we were on a ledge, and there were no other climbers to be seen. The probability of a fall was high, and the consequences of said fall would have been awful. It was a long way down. The time was 4 p.m. Two hours of daylight remained.

By now I was coming up with all sorts of positive-thinking platitudes. "Way to go guys, you are doing great. 'Can't' is a bad word. The worst is behind us. Not much farther to go."

Joe told me to "stop the propaganda."

After what seemed like an eternity, we made it off the loose rock and into the snow. It was then that the guides proved their worth. Young men such as Joe and Tommy typically respond better to a male leader who is not their father. This is particularly true if the leader in question is younger and more dashing than their dad. (I set a low standard for both youth and dashingness.) True to form, Tommy seemed to respond much better to Rodrigo's gentle Spanish encouragement than to my feeble motivational psychobabble.

The guides demonstrated how to glissade down the snow, using the ice axe as a brake. The mood of the kids immediately brightened. We slid down the first hill and they hopped up, with a little more spring in their steps now. Onto the second hill—not as steep as the first—and they were beginning to smile. Next, the big ice-covered hill for a fast trip down, and soon they were laughing once again. It was then that I realized everything was going to be okay.

As I look back on the day, I truly believe that Rodrigo and Sebastian were carefully observing Joe and Tommy all the way up the mountain. When the boys kept up a good pace and didn't complain, they decided we had a chance to make the summit and get down safely. Had they thought otherwise, I feel certain they would have advised us to turn back. They were skilled, patient climbers, and we are very grateful to them. When we reached the bottom, they gave us hugs as if we had just conquered Mt. Everest.

So, was this day hike a good idea? Well, the kids learned how to use crampons and an ice axe to ascend a snow-covered peak and how to glissade down. These are nice outdoor skills to have. They learned that they hate the smell of brimstone, so the thought of an eternity in hell is now more frightening than it was before. Perhaps most importantly, they learned that most of the limits they place on themselves are in their minds. They learned how to reach beyond their known capabilities and to carry on, even when things were horrible.

Still, I now know that this is not somewhere I should have led my children. This did not occur to me until we were already on the way down the volcano. Had I been the person in charge of the hike, I feel certain that I would have figured it out on the way up.

In truth, I was in charge. I just didn't realize it. I know my own safety standards. I abandoned those standards and allowed the guides' judgment to supersede my own. My assumption that the guides would know best was based on this: I paid them, so they were the designated leaders and therefore the experts. This was a mistake, because my first job as a father is to protect my children. In this instance that would have meant paying constant attention to our safety and then challenging any decision that put us in danger. I failed to do that. The fact that we returned unharmed does not make it right. Our safe descent is tribute to my sons' gumption, not my leadership.

The following day a change came over the family. During our year of travel, returning home had always seemed far away, off in the distance. But now it was only two weeks away and because it was near, anticipation occupied our thoughts. Earlier in the trip, whenever we hit a rough spot we would always fall back on the routine of school, but now we found it difficult to concentrate.

Chile is a wonderful county, but we had lost the requisite passion to appreciate its beauty. We were homesick.

CHAPTER 15

HOME AT LAST

Untold Tales, Lessons Learned, Lives Changed |

We decided to return home a week early. Jill had this to say:

> *I couldn't wait to see my parents. From the moment we said goodbye in Idaho, I wondered if this would be the last time I would see one or both of them. I wanted to surprise them by coming home early. But it's not like I want to resume our old way of life. I just want to go home for a week, hug everybody and then get back on the road.*

I set to work planning the final leg of the trip. We could fly standby from Santiago, Chile, to Atlanta for free, but the airline that would take us from Atlanta to Phoenix wanted an additional $350 per ticket. It just didn't seem right.

Jill wanted to pay the difference and be done with it, but I told her that emotion does not affect my sense of value. We had just traveled through six continents, changed numerous plane tickets without paying a nickel, and now we were supposed to pay $1,750 to change a ticket from Atlanta to Phoenix? I suggested that we fly to Atlanta and see what happens. Jill was angry. "What if we can't get to Phoenix?" she asked. "Are we going to stay in Atlanta for a week?"

I agreed that would be terrible. Neither of us could imagine a more disappointing end to a trip around the world. I continued to research our options, including a one-way van rental, alternate flights, trains, even the Greyhound bus. None seemed to work.

That night we went out for empanadas. Cognac was on sale for fifty cents a glass. I don't particularly like cognac, but I love a good sale. I drank two dollars worth. By the time we walked back to our hotel, a week in Atlanta had become a wonderful option. We could watch the Atlanta Braves! Tour the Coca-Cola factory! Re-create Sherman's march to the sea! Why, Atlanta would be the cherry atop the sundae, the perfect exclamation point to complete our trip!

Apart from a bad hangover, I thought the flight from Santiago to Atlanta went fine. After 245 days, we found ourselves back in the U.S.A. I approached the airline counter to try to talk them into making our flight change for free. I was no longer anxious, thanks to my cognac-inspired scheme devised the night before. If they said "no," we would be happy to simply rent a car and tour the American South for a week.

"No" was exactly what they said, so I tried another angle: "Have you heard anything about that volcano that just erupted in Chile?"

"Oh, yes," the agent said. "I saw that on CNN. It looked bad."

"Well, that's because it was bad—we were right near there, and things were a little dicey." Technically, this was true. Things were more than a little dicey for the people and cattle near the volcano, just not for us. "We decided to leave early," I added. This was also true, albeit unrelated to the volcano. The agent called over his supervisor and explained the situation. The supervisor said that because we were fleeing a natural disaster, the airline would change our tickets to Phoenix free of charge.

As we boarded the plane to Phoenix, we told the flight attendant that this was the final flight of our seventeen-country, one-year trip around the world. We expected that she would make an announcement, which would have thrilled the kids, but she never did.

It was 102 degrees when we landed at Phoenix Sky Harbor Airport. We drove to Grandma and Grandpa's house, and instead of knocking, we just walked in. Grandpa was wearing only his underwear and talking on the phone—not quite the scene we had imagined.

After two weeks at home, Tommy, Cami, and I traveled north to our cabin in Ketchikan, Alaska. Joe stayed in Mesa to take Latin in summer school, and Jill stayed with him until class ended in early July. The two of them then flew to Ketchikan to join us, where we spent a cold, rainy summer with lots of time to reflect on our year of travel. It was the closest I have ever felt to my family.

Soon it was August—time to return to Mesa and get back to work. In 2007, Mesa was described in *The Economist* as "the quintessential low-slung sub-urban city. Mile after mile of strip malls and tract houses, whose evocative names and fanciful arches cannot disguise the fact that they are large, stucco-covered boxes." In 2008, Mesa was voted third-most-boring city in the United States. Paradoxically, ranking third is more boring than being voted most boring. If you are most boring, at least you have won an award, but as the bronze medal winner, instead of wishing for more excitement in Mesa, I wondered just what it would take to be number one.

Mesa had seemed just fine before we left on our trip, but upon our return, we noticed the bland nature of the town. In truth, Mesa had not changed while we were away, but I sure had. When I looked in the mirror, I was greyer and much fatter. For the first time in my life I was embarrassed about my appearance.

One night we met some friends at a sports bar. I was telling travel stories and after a few minutes I noticed the boredom on their faces and watched as their eyes moved from me to the wall of big screen TVs that featured a swimming race from the 2008 Beijing Summer Olympics. Watching the Olympics was a different experience than before the trip. We still cheered for the United States, but mostly we found ourselves cheering for countries we liked and rooting against countries we didn't. Jill noticed me watching the swim race and asked who I wanted to win.

"The Japanese guy," I answered.

"Let me guess—you want the Italian swimmer to drown," she replied.

"Not quite. But I do want him to wind up in last place and then get short-changed when he tries to buy chop suey in the Olympic Village."

The following night at dinner, I warned the kids not to bore their friends with travel stories. Joe chuckled.

"What is so funny?" I asked.

"Dad, you bore people with travel stories all the time," Joe replied.

He was right, of course. I am introverted by nature and terrible when it comes to small talk—this makes me like most other doctors and it also makes me unexciting at parties. Before the trip, when we would be on our way to a party, Jill would remind me to "try to be a little more sociable," but now she said, "could you just quit talking about the trip all the time?"

"I finally feel like I have something interesting to talk about," I said. "And it's not that I want to brag about the places we have been—far from it. I want to tell people how travel brought us closer together as a family. I want them to know that the bickering kids do at the start of a journey goes away after a few days. I want to tell them that the world is a safer place than we have been led to believe. I want to encourage them to go and see it."

Jill had realized right away that travel tales have a tendency to bore people, and she was more low key in her approach:

The only people that I felt truly loved hearing about our escapades were my family. At least at length. Most people just want to hear about one or two little stories. At least that is what I think.

I love to talk about the trip, but I don't want to bore anyone who really is not interested. It's like when a four-year-old asks, "Where do babies come from?" versus a nine-year-old asking the same question. When people ask about the trip, I tried to gauge how to answer. I still don't feel very close to my closest friends. I feel closest to my family.

When it was time to return to work, I was nervous. I hadn't cared for a sick person for fourteen months. I was worried that the requisite knowledge to practice medicine would be absent. I was pleasantly surprised by how easily I got back into the groove. Much of medicine is heuristic, relying on pattern recognition to make a diagnosis, and once learned, this is not easily forgotten.

One of the most difficult parts of returning to work was being away from the family for ten hours at a time. After fourteen months with the five of us together constantly, you might think I would welcome some variety. Nothing could be further from the truth. When I was away at work, I had a real sense of loss. I pined for my family.

At work, some people asked about the trip and some did not. At first, I was taken aback at this apparent lack of curiosity. I had just gone around the world. Didn't people want to know about it? But as I look back, I understand. We didn't go to Disneyland for a weekend; we went around the world for a year. The typical question you ask a returning traveler—"How was the trip?"—was as awkward to ask as it was difficult to answer.

People did ask questions. They asked what my favorite place was, and how it was to be back. Remembering how I had bored my friends at the sports bar, I gave brief, clichéd answers. If I noticed genuine interest, my answers became longer, but I always tried to watch for signs of boredom.

Some of the more specific questions seemed designed to confirm preconceived notions.

Question: "Did you feel threatened by Islamic terrorists?"

My answer: "No. The Muslims we met couldn't have been more gracious and they were well aware we were from America. In fact, during our year of travel we did not hear a single anti-American comment."

Question: "Aren't the French stuck up?"

My answer: "It's difficult to make generalizations. We weren't in France long enough to become cultural insiders. They were nice to us."

Question: "Don't you feel blessed to be home back to the best country on earth and don't your kids have more of an appreciation now than when you left?"

Answer: "Our trip across America was great. I love our country, but we don't have the best of many things: food, cell phones, domestic airlines—to name but a few. Furthermore, when we left people were campaigning for president. We were gone a year and they still have three months of campaigning to go! That is unique, ridiculous, and awful."

One day, someone asked a really good question: "How did being apart for a year change the way you view the U.S.?"

Answer: "It changed it a lot. We are the hardest working, most optimistic people on earth. During our year of travel, we met so many people who wanted to move to America, to be Americans, to raise their children as Americans. When you think about that, you realize it is unique in history; Tommy could move to Japan, but he would never be considered Japanese, nor would his children, nor would his grandchildren. But if a Japanese man moves to the U.S., takes a citizenship exam in which he pledges to obey and honor the ideas articulated by Madison and Jefferson, he will be as American as anyone who came over on the Mayflower. This is why the Statue of Liberty is such an important symbol and beacon of hope, especially to people that live in tyrannies such as Burma—a country I am proud to say my children chose not to visit."

Now that I am back home, it matters less whether our ship of state tacks left or right; we are constantly tinkering with this and probably always will. What matters is that our Founding Fathers constructed a sublime democracy that honors the rights of man and has prospered for 240 years—the longest in history.

After a few months at home, I asked Jill what the transition was like for her. Here is her response:

Being home is quite boring and monotonous. This is not something that I can say to anyone without feeling like I am criticizing their lives, so I keep to myself more now than before, I think. I look at this trip as such an incredible gift, a gift that I have a hard time sharing because it is so different and personal. A gift that has changed the way I feel about the everyday job of living life. A gift that has me wondering what I do about that feeling when it is what I have to do now. Stay home, finish raising the kids. . . . I know it's just like India . . . love it or hate it. . . . it is temporary and I must at least grasp it and appreciate it.

As for me, I found myself not wanting to be around old friends and not having the energy to make new ones. I started drinking more—anything but cognac. Some days I would lie in bed until noon, thinking about the trip, and Jill was right there with me. Our *annus mirabilis* was over. On bad days—and there were many—it seemed as though the one great accomplishment of our lives was now behind us and all that remained was day after day of drudgery.

Around this time, our dear friend, Father Jerry Welsch, sent us the following e-mail: "Congratulations on completing your journey around the world. The challenge now will be to find meaning in the day-to-day."

For help with this, we turned to our children. Nostalgia is the domain of adults. Children live in the present. The kids were still open to newness, still excitable, grateful, joyful. Field trips to local museums that to our adult minds would have suffered by comparison were still wondrous to our kids, because they did not feel compelled to compare them. Rather than saying, "The Mesa Arts Center is nowhere near as good as the Louvre," the kids said, "The Mesa Arts Center is cool. A lady there showed us a sculpture like the ones we saw on the trip."

Just as the man from the school district had predicted, the kids were fine academically. For Tommy, there were some behavioral bumps in the road. His fifth-grade teacher, Mr. Lorenzen, had this to say:

Tommy did have a few struggles adapting to the classroom environment. He is a very smart boy and was filled with enthusiasm during class discussions. . . . Tommy free wrote wonderfully . . . journals, stories and personal narratives. He struggled with the organization and elaboration within his writing.

It was hard for him to wait for a turn as we had 33 other students and I could see the frustration it caused him when being reminded to wait. He struggled most in loose classroom setting: P.E. and recess. He tended to be out of control when supervision was sparse. . . . He did improve immensely on these areas as the year progressed.

Charitably, Mr. Lorenzen chose not to mention that Tommy looked like a ragamuffin. Still traumatized by his experience in Turkey, Tommy refused to get his hair cut and he also refused to change his clothes, insisting on wearing the same sweatshirt and pants every day. During the trip when more dirty clothes meant more time in laundromats we had praised this behavior as "efficiency," so it was hard to correct it now.

Cami struggled a little too, but with shyness, not rowdiness. Her third-grade teacher, Mrs. Silva, made these comments:

> *Cami began the year with excitement and a little nervousness. She was anxious to see her friends, but seemed to do a lot of watching of classmates. Cami was ready to share her experiences from the very beginning but sometimes needed to be encouraged. She was always watching me to make sure I approved of what she was doing and didn't hesitate to ask questions.*

Whenever Cami's class studied something related to the trip, I would ask whether our travels came up. One day, Cami replied, "Every time we talk about another country, the whole class turns around and stares at me."

"How does that make you feel?" I asked.

"Fine," she replied, and walked toward the new puppy. Cami had specific memories of the trip but no clue as to the magnitude of the experience as a whole, just as you would expect from an eight-year-old.

Joe's return to everyday life was more existential, though I don't think that is the word he would use to describe it. One day I was waiting to pick him up. I noticed him walking out of school, shaking his head. "How was school today, Joe," I asked.

"Terrible. They are such idiots—they are so shallow."

"Your teachers?"

"No," he said. "They are great, I love them. It's my classmates that suck. Idiots, idiots, idiots! They won't shut up. They talk constantly and write stupid notes while I am trying to listen to the teacher and learn something."

"Do they make fart noises?" I asked.

"No. . . . What does that have to do with anything?"

"Never mind. I just was wondering."

When it came to schoolwork, Joe was a different kid. We no longer had to ask him to do his homework. His eighth-grade history book featured photos of Pompeii, Normandy, and Istanbul, and I realized just how much of an advantage our travels had given him. For every other student in that class, these were far-off places of no importance, except as a correct answer to a test question. To Joey they were real places with real people. What happened there—the battles, the cemeteries, the architecture—all meant something to him.

Money also took on a different meaning for Joe. It had become a means to an end, not an end in itself, and for this we were pleased. One day Joe was watching the game show *Deal or No Deal* and the "deal price" got up to $170,000. Until that moment, Joe had been opposed to taking the deal. Suddenly he said, "That guy should take the money."

"Why now?" I asked, thinking the answer would pertain to probability.

"That's trip money," he replied.

"What would you do if you had that money?" I asked.

"Travel again—only I would go at a faster pace."

I took this opportunity to ask whether he would like to be an exchange student.

"Yes!" He replied. "As soon as possible for as long as possible."

"How would you feel about going somewhere to help the poor? Like Tanzania or India?" I asked.

"I'd rather go somewhere nice, like New Zealand or Japan."

It is human nature to choose the pleasant over the difficult, so I understood, yet I was troubled by this answer and I mentioned it to Jill. "Why does that bother you?" she asked.

I responded, "As a teenager I would have chosen to do volunteer work in a poor country because I really believed that I could change the whole world with acts of kindness."

"Where did that lead you?"

"I no longer think I can change the whole world, but I believe more than ever that I can help my little corner of it," I said. "Joe knows that the world is a big place, unlikely to be changed by him, so in that respect I think that our journey robbed him of idealism."

Jill replied, "He is fourteen years old—a little young to be drawing conclusions."

"I just wish we had done medical missionary work in Tanzania," I said. "We had the chance. By dedicating part of the trip to service, we could have led by example."

Jill replied, "We discussed missionary work, and if you remember I wanted to go more than you did. We decided not to go, to protect the kids from seeing all that suffering and death. Plus, it would have been a logistical nightmare. What would the kids have done while we were working all day? Those arguments are as sound now as they were a year ago."

"The kids would have found a way to deal with the hardship."

"I agree with you there," said Jill. "They are more adaptable than I ever would have thought. Look at how well they have adapted to being back home, while you and I still struggle."

After a year back in school, Joe became part of the "mindless conversations" during class—so much so that it earned him a few detentions. He had become friends with some of the "shallow idiots" he had previously criticized. Silently, I questioned his sincerity in some of these actions, and therein lies the rub. His options were to either become part of the adolescent subculture or put his head down and wait for it to pass. Sensing that it could be a long wait, Joe came to the realization that the trip was over, and it was time to move on. Slowly, Jill and I came to this realization too.

And so we stumble onward, still struggling to find meaning in the day-to-day. Though the trip ended, all those days and nights in other lands live on through memories and stories.

Today an electronic picture frame in our kitchen randomly displays our trip photos. Just as the kids never had to be reminded to ask for their dollar snack when we were on the road, none of us has to be reminded where the pictures were taken. Each photo, as it flashes by, brings to mind a different tale from our year of adventure.

ACKNOWLEDGMENTS

A t a little league game, a journalist friend of mine named Mark Moran tapped me on the shoulder and said, "You need to write a book about your trip." Mark inspired me and then guided me through the early stages of the writing process. Without him this book would not exist.

My dear friends John Kelly and Tom Moffo read some of the chapters early on when they were very rough. I am grateful for their thoughtful and honest feedback. Thanks also to Julia Kelly (no relation to John) for her comments when the manuscript was in its later stages.

Josh Stevens at Reedy Press Publishing convinced me that publishing a "collection of essays" as I had originally intended was weak minded and lazy (my words, not his). Once I had done the work of tying the chapters together, he introduced me to Pat Corrigan. Pat edited this manuscript twice. The first go-round she shredded my chapters and thickened my skin. The second time she inspired me to see the book through to its end. Then she sent me back to Josh who along with Matt Heidenry (both SLUH '91) created the book you now hold in your hands. Thank you Pat, Josh, and Matt.

My darling and increasingly beautiful bride, who is patient and kind with all living creatures, was especially patient with me while I sat in a rocking chair for two years writing this book. Thank you! You are the love of my life.

BIBLIOGRAPHY

Chapter 1

Bergreen, Laurence. *Over the Edge of the World: Magellan's Terrifying Circumnavigation of the Globe*. New York: Harper Collins, 2003.

Chapter 2

Hassbrouck, Edward. *Practical Nomad: How to Travel around the World*. Berkeley, Calif.: Avalon Travel Publishing, 2004.

Hess, Daniel J. *The Whole World Guide to Culture Learning*. Boston: Intercultural Press, 1994.

Times Books World Weather Guide. New York: Times Books, 1990.

Chapter 6

Duffy, Eamon. *Saints and Sinners: A History of the Popes*. New Haven, Conn.: Yale University Press, 2006.

Manchester, William. *A World Lit Only by Fire*. New York: Little Brown, 1994.

Nicholl, Charles. *Leonardo da Vinci: Flights of the Mind*. New York: Viking, Penguin, 2004.

Chapter 7

Twain, Mark. *The Innocents Abroad*. New York: Signet Classics, 1990.

Chapter 8

Wood, Michael. *The Story of India*. New York: Random House, 2008.

Chapter 9

Handley, Paul M. *The King Never Smiles*. New Haven, Conn.: Yale University Press, 2006.

Chapter 11

Thomas, Nicholas. *Discoveries: The Voyages of Captain Cook*. New York: Penguin Books, 2004.

Lansing, Alfred. *Endurance: Shackleton's Incredible Voyage*. New York: Carroll & Graf, 1999.

Worsley, F. A. *Shackleton's Boat Journey*. New York: W.W. Norton, 1977.

Chapter 12

McLauchlan, Gordon. *A Short History of New Zealand*. New York: Penguin, 2004.

Chapter 15

Storti, Craig. *The Art of Coming Home*. Boston: Intercultural Press, 2003.

PIZZA RESULTS

*S*ome things can be made just as delicious at home as in a restaurant, but pizza is not one of them. To create a truly great pizza requires not only great ingredients but a dedicated pizza oven. Having traveled the entire world on a quest for the greatest pizza, I can now confidently say that the greatest pizza on earth is made right here in America. We tried pizza in every country we visited (except Dubai). Pizza in other countries tends to be low on sauce and skimpy on ingredients, hence only four international pizzas made the list—all in the bottom half.

1. Gino's pizza (pepperoni and mushroom), Chicago. The only deep dish pizza on the list. Cornbread-type crust that is unique and just incredible. Tangy sauce, good cheese. They didn't skimp on the ingredients.

2. Squan Tavern, Manasquan, New Jersey. Meatball and mushroom pizza. Tastiest meatballs on earth perfectly spiced and baked instead of fried so they are not in the least bit greasy. Sliced thin on top of good sauce and thin crust.

3. Turoni's pizza, Evansville, Indiana. Best thin crust ever—mediocre sauce (not tart enough).

4. Imo's Pizza, St. Louis (pepperoni and bacon). My mouth waters just thinking about it. Thin, crisp crust; provel cheese (is there anywhere but St. Louis that has provel?); and bacon does not mean bacon bits, it means big slices of bacon cooked along with the pizza.

5. Basbeaux's pizza, Broadripple, Indiana. Quatto formaggio with bacon and mushroom. Eclectic but delicious—riccotta cheese and bacon, a great combination.

6. Pizzeria: Pan Pan. Dormelletto, Italy. Salami and extra cheese, extra sauce. Wood-fired, thin-crust pizza, excellent flavor. We added the extra cheese and sauce when we returned to the restaurant the second time and continued to request this whenever ordering pizza in Italy.

7. Waterfront Pizza, Port Townsend, Washington. Coppa and sun-dried tomatoes. Great sourdough crust, tangy sauce, and a large helping of ingredients.

8. Pizzeria Del Mundo, Bariloche, Argentina. Ham and cheese pizza—delicious cured ham and tart sauce make this a winner.

9. Hell Pizza, Christchurch, New Zealand. Mushroom pizza (it was Friday during lent so we didn't have any meat toppings). Excellent crust.

10. Pizzedelic Cartier. Quebec City, Canada. LeGarnier pizza: cappicola, mushrooms, green peppers. One of Tommy's favorites. Great sauce.